CHESHIRE

Secrets from the Past

Rodger Burgess

SIGMA Leisure

Reprinted with minor corrections 2002

Published by Sigma Leisure – an imprint of
Sigma Press, 1 South Oak Lane, Wilmslow, Cheshire SK9 6AR, England.

British Library Cataloguing in Publication Data
A CIP record for this book is available from the British Library.

ISBN: 1-85058-728-0

Typesetting and Design by: Sigma Press, Wilmslow, Cheshire.

Cover Design: Design House

Cover photographs: restored cross at Gawsworth Church

Printed by: MFP Design & Print

Foreword

In the po-faced, self-absorbed, politically correct climate of the early 21st century, there doesn't seem to be much room for the eccentric, or the oddity. What happened to the "just fancy that" response to the tall tale, magical myth, or local legend? Rodger Burgess sets out to redress that balance with a vengeance.

Visit here the weird goings on of Mother Redcap who looked after the booty of the Mersey privateers, and left hidden treasure somewhere between Wallasey and New Brighton. Absorb the glamour of "Cheshire's answer to Hollywood," the Oval sports ground in Bebington which became the Paris Olympic stadium for *Chariots of Fire*.

And be amazed by the Wizard's Well at Alderley Edge, associated with King Arthur where the visitor is welcomed with the legend. "Drink of this and take thy fill, for the water falls by the Wizard's will." Wow.

This is no dry-as-dust succession of monarchs, wars and disasters. This is history with her tongue in her cheek, a smile on her face, and amazement in her eyes. It is also a useful handbook for arranging outings to outlandish and unusual venues.

Seven thousand years of "life" in Cheshire: *Cheshire Life*, a mere youngster of 66 years, has got to be amused, amazed and agog at that.

Patrick O'Neill
Editor, Cheshire Life

Dedication

To my wife Marion, who has spent many hours with me in graveyards and other places collecting material for the book, our children David and Diane, who have had to listen to endless "discoveries" and my mother Anne, who inspired in me a love of Wirral. It is written in the hope that our grandchildren Morgan and Cody will also learn to appreciate all that surrounds us and enjoy the secrets of the past.

Preface

I was born in Bootle, now considered part of Liverpool, but moved to Wirral as a child and have lived in Cheshire ever since. For over thirty years I served in The Cheshire Constabulary working and living in many parts of the county. As with many Officers of my generation I spent a great deal of time talking to the public, drinking tea and picking up many "Oddities" or pieces of apparently useless information about the county and people. I hasten to add that a "Bobbie's Job" was far from being all tea and chat!

It was only later that I realised that these "Oddities" were not useless at all but were Keys into the past and opened a fascinating opportunity to look at the story of the county and people of Cheshire. This story was far from being the boring history I had previously thought but was rich in interest, stimulating thought and a more active and questioning approach to an afternoons walk or drive.

In reality, living in Cheshire is like living in the middle of a book. All around are stories and facts, many of which are of great interest, but unless we read the other pages, we will never truly appreciate our surroundings. The buildings and places that we pass each day form an index to a story more fascinating than we could ever read, because we are all part of that story.

Looking over the Cheshire countryside on a sunny day, it is difficult, if not impossible, to appreciate that the county has a very different past from the peaceful picture laid out before us. Imagine a country riven by war. The whole social structure destroyed by invaders who remained in occupation for several hundred years before being replaced by a volatile mix of local war lords and expanding distant powers until yet another occupier took control and launched a murderous campaign to destroy all opposition.

Those of the population who survived the terror then continued to exist in a border country caught in a power struggle between two independent countries, drawing men to war and suffering battles and campaigns on its fields for further centuries. Alongside the decimation of war rode another threat, quieter but more deadly. Disease and plague sweeping town and countryside alike, killing without regard to rank or religion. Would you like to live in such a place? The country I have described above is our own fair county of Cheshire.

Lying alongside the present boundary with Wales, Cheshire has long played an important role in the relationship between England and Wales. Before the Norman invasion, the county formed the boundary between the Kingdoms of Mercia and Northumbria. Then, during the ninth and tenth centuries, the Vikings, who exercised considerable influence over all those parts of Europe accessible either by sea or from the rivers, settled in Wirral and along the high ground in the east of the county. All have left their mark.

Hidden Cheshire is an attempt to look at some of the more unusual Keys to our past which can be found around every corner. Arranged in geographical areas rather than in subjects, this book aims to encourage people to examine their surroundings and to question how the present county of Cheshire came to be created in its present form.

At the end of each Chapter there are map references for the more unusual subjects which have appeared in the text. To simplify matters, references are not given for towns and villages. All references are to Ordnance Survey Maps.

Contents

Chapter One
Cheshire as part of the story of Britain 1
The Evidence of 8,000 Years of History

Chapter Two
The City of Chester 7
The Roman Legacy, the City Walls and Prison, the Port, Railways and the New Cut

Chapter Three
The West of the Wirral Peninsula and the Chester Ports 13
Shotwick, Burton, Denhall, Neston, Parkgate, Gayton, Heswall and Thurstaston

Chapter Four
The Wirral Coast and Islands 26
Irby, Thurstaston, Greasby, Caldy, West Kirby, The Hilbre Islands, Hoylake and Meols, Leasowe and New Brighton

Chapter Five
Maritime Cheshire 37
Bidston, Liscard, Birkenhead, Tranmere, Rock Ferry, Thornton Hough, Brimstage, Eastham, Willaston and Ellesmere Port

Chapter Six
The Border with Wales 52
Farndon, Shocklach, Bickerton, Tushingham, Peckforton, Tarporley, Nantwich, Audlem and Combermere

Chapter Seven
Salt and the growth of Religion 61
Middlewich, Winsford, Vale Royal, Sandbach, Barthomley, Hassall Green, Mow Cop and Congleton

Chapter Eight
Eastern Cheshire and Tablets of Stone 71
Marton, Gawsworth, Macclesfield, The Macclesfield Canal, Bollington, Disley and Prestbury

Chapter Nine
From The Bronze Age to The Space Age 81
Jodrell Bank, Wilmslow, Alderley Edge, Chelford, Mobberley, Holmes Chapel, Byley, Cranage and Toft

Chapter Ten
Roman Roads, Parachutes and Children's Stories 92
Knutsford, Tatton Park, Mere, Appleton Thorn, Thelwall, Wilderspool, Warrington, Daresbury and Runcorn

Chapter Eleven
The Industrial Revolution and Modern Communications. 100
Road and Canal Systems and the village of Hale.

Chapter Twelve
The Centre of the County 105
Northwich, Bostock, Great Budworth, Little Budworth, Eddisbury, Delamere and Nunsmere.

Concluding Thoughts 111

Bibliography 112

Chapter One

Cheshire as part of the story of Britain

The Evidence of 8,000 Years of History

The county of Cheshire does not have a high profile. Many people, despite having lived in the county all their lives, find it hard to name a single time or event in which Cheshire has played an important part in the history of Britain. In reality the county has made a significant contribution to the history of England, Wales, Scotland and Ireland and continues to do so.

The archers of Cheshire were for several centuries famous and feared throughout the world for their loyalty and fighting ability. Richard II, distrusting many of those who surrounded him, chose the men of Cheshire to form his personal bodyguard, a task they seem to have undertaken with considerable enthusiasm as they managed to upset a considerable number of courtiers. In today's world, when everybody has to be politically correct, this is surely an ability to be admired and nurtured!

On a sunny day, walkers strolling along the sea front at Meols in Wirral pass a submerged forest lying under the sand and the site of one of the earliest settlements in Cheshire. Although not seen for several decades, the forest appears from time to time, giving a hint of a peninsula very different from the one we see today. A rise in the sea level and erosion of the soft sandstone rock has resulted in considerable changes to the ancient coastline, which appears to have extended much further into Liverpool Bay.

Items and relicts found at Meols indicate that men occupied the area between 5000 and 8000 years ago. More recent finds suggest that the location was the site of a Roman port or settlement of which no trace remains.

Further evidence of the early inhabitants of Cheshire can be found near Congleton where a small sign on the road between Congleton and Rushton Spencer indicates the Neolithic tomb of 'The Bridestones', built some four to five thousand years ago. In many places throughout Cheshire you can find Tumuli, which are large

The Bridestones Neolithic burial chamber, near Congleton

man-made mounds dating from the Bronze Age. Many of the mounds were burial chambers and these, together with traces of settlements from that period, enable us to form some ideas about the way our ancestors lived, and the customs that were followed when they died.

A modern day murder hunt in Wilmslow during the early 1980s resulted in the discovery of "Wilmslow Pete" the victim of a ritual murder some 2500 years ago. The discovery of his body, together with a female skull found nearby, provided an intriguing insight into the more violent aspects of life before the arrival of the Romans. As with many similar discoveries more questions are raised than resolved.

About 500BC the Celts arrived from Europe and gradually populated the whole of the country with the Cornovii tribe living in the area we now know as Cheshire. It was about this time that the forts of Helsby, Bickerton, Oakmere and Eddisbury were constructed. This was the start of a period of considerable population movement across the whole of Europe as it was only some 500 years later, in AD43, that the Romans arrived in the south of England after two failed attempts at invasion and gradually moved northwards.

Once the Roman army had established control in the south they required bases further north to continue their expansion into Wales and the north of Britain. In AD45 they began the building of a legion-

The Roman bridge over the River Dee at Chester

ary fort at Chester introducing a whole new social structure and in so doing laid the foundations of modern society and the first outline of what would later become the county of Cheshire.

For several centuries after the Romans left Britain in AD410 the society they had established appears to have continued in a modified form with the local British, or Celts managing quite well. Unfortunately fresh visitors from Europe appeared and the Anglo Saxons gained control of large parts of the British Isles creating separate Kingdoms which later resulted in conflict.

Two of the largest Kingdoms began pushing towards the Cheshire area. From the midlands, Mercia began to expand in the direction of Wales whilst from the north-east the powerful Kingdom of Northumbria also began to move against the strength of the Welsh. At this time it is probable that Cheshire formed part of the Kingdom of Powys and as such was directly in the line of advance taken by the Northumbrian army. Matters came to a head in AD613 when a large army from Northumbria travelled south and defeated the British forces in a battle near Chester during which there was considerable loss of life and much of the city destroyed.

Bangor-on-Dee, a few miles south of Chester, was the location of a large monastery and teaching centre important not only to the local tribes but to others much farther afield. The monks appeared to have played an active role in supporting the army, with the result that the victorious Northumbrian intruders selected them for attention.

The monastery and all trace of the great religious site were totally destroyed.

Following their successful campaign the Northumbrian army withdrew but Cheshire was still under pressure from Mercia. At first the Mercian army joined with the British to eliminate the danger from Northumbria, but then, the Mercians themselves expanded into what is now Cheshire and began to push against the Welsh. This was the start of the Welsh wars although the full ferocity only erupted after the Norman invasion. It was the Mercian King Offa who constructed the famous Dyke, the full purpose of which is not known but it is believed to have been a boundary or perimeter against the Welsh rather than a full defensive wall.

During the 9th and 10th centuries, Viking raids were spreading across all the coastlines of Europe. Not content with the sea coasts, Vikings ships penetrated many of the larger river systems spreading fear and chaos as far as Russia. At a time when few countries maintained large armies and those that did were unable to mobilise them quickly, the appearance of a large group of extremely violent invaders must have spread terror and unsettled the established monarchs. Chester was sacked by Danish Vikings in AD893 and by their cousins from the Isle of Man in AD980.

Most of the invaders in the west of the county were Irish-Norse, the same people who had occupied Ireland and the Isle of Man. The Norsemen originated in what is now Scandinavia with the name 'Viking' meaning the 'Sea Kings' a term normally associated with the sea raiders from the northern area we call Norway. The east of the county also suffered from Norse intruders, but these were the Danes who controlled large parts of the east of England, which had fallen under the authority of the Danish King. The strength of the Danish invasion and settlements can be seen in the 11th century when Canute, King of all England between AD1016 and AD1029, ruled not only England but also Denmark and Norway. Legend states that it was from him that the name 'Knutsford' comes.

Today their legacy can be traced in village names. Thingwall, Thurstaston, and those names ending in 'by' such as Greasby, Frankby or West Kirby, indicate an Irish-Norse influence. The ending 'Hulme', such as Cheadle Hulme or Church Hulme (Holmes Chapel), and the names of Toft and possibly Rostherne, appear to be the legacy of the Danish Vikings who spread from the East.

The very real threat posed by these Viking raids caused the old Iron Age forts at Eddisbury, Bickerton and other Cheshire locations to be re-fortified in AD914 to defend against them.

The Norman invasion in 1066 was to make far reaching changes to the society that had previously existed although the new "Shires" in many ways were based on the old counties which had been set up under the Mercian Kingdom.

Norman rule was not welcomed with open arms and in 1069 a widespread revolt erupted in northern England including Cheshire. William did not reach the position of King by being soft and the uprising was crushed with great force and loss of life, with many parts of Cheshire and the neighbouring counties being laid waste. The Domesday Book shows many farms and villages as uninhabited after the revolt was suppressed.

Under Norman rule Cheshire, positioned as it was between England and Wales, greatly increased in importance. At first the county included Flintshire, parts of Denbighshire, Lancashire as far north as the river Ribble and parts of the Yorkshire Dales. In the 12th century Lancashire was reformed, like Cheshire it had been a county before 1066 and Flintshire ceased to be part of Cheshire after 1284. Until 1974 the county boundaries remained almost unchanged.

The wars with Wales, which continued for several centuries, have left many traces in the county especially in Wirral and near to Chester. Cheshire was a "County Palatine" meaning that it enjoyed an almost independent authority to manage its own affairs under the Royal Earl. This independence included the right to levy its own taxes and administer its own courts. This power was retained until 1536 and was a direct acknowledgement of the county's strategic importance.

The archers of Cheshire often formed the "artillery" of the English armies as they fought in the many wars against European powers and in the many clashes within this country. They were renowned for being able to release a devastating storm of arrows, which could shatter an opposing force before they could even approach to within range of the sword.

All war is terrible, but perhaps the worst of all is civil war that divides families and pits brother against brother. The struggle for power in the 15th century lead to the Wars of the Roses between the houses of Lancashire and Yorkshire and divided the loyalty of the men of Cheshire. Many men from the county died at Blore Heath near Shrewsbury and other battles, with families fighting for opposing sides.

The civil war in the 17th century ravaged many parts of the county, and active participation in the trial and execution of King Charles was just one event that involved Cheshire. Many of our churches still show signs of the fighting, whilst puritan zeal lead to the destruction of many ancient symbols and windows.

It is easy to imagine that one of the major causes of death in the past was war and yet in truth disease extracted a much greater toll from a population suffering from a poor diet, a lack of hygiene and the lack of a proper means to combat illness. As the population of the country grew and trade increased so plague and epidemics spread causing suffering and death. Traces of the attempts to combat the danger can be found mingling with evidence of the earlier invaders and the growth of religion.

In more modern times, Cheshire has continued to play its part in the development of Great Britain. There is much to remind us of the Industrial Revolution, especially the development of the canals, roads and railways that proved so vital in the provision of transport between the factories and ports of the north-west.

Chapter Two

The City of Chester

The Roman Legacy, the City Walls and Prison, the Port, Railways and the New Cut

Chester was important to the Romans because of its position at the highest crossing point on the river and its harbour. Home to the Second Legion and then the Twentieth Legion, the City was vital for the war against the Welsh and also acted as the centre of trade for Ireland and much of the West.

Although much of the "Tudor" appearance belongs to a later period there are some fascinating traces of earlier centuries. Large sections of the City Wall were built in mediaeval times, which suffered considerably during the civil war when the city was under siege. However, in several places, sections of the original Roman fortification can be found.

There are many ruins to remind us of the Roman occupation. One of the least obvious gives a deeper insight into the personality of the individual soldier and is to be found on the south side of the river. In a small park bordering the riverbank is a shrine to the Roman goddess, Minerva. The carving of the goddess, with an owl alongside, survived relatively intact for centuries until in recent years mindless vandalism has caused considerable damage. Several other altars have been recovered indicating that the Romans had a selection of Gods servicing the spiritual needs of their legions, which were manned by soldiers from many countries. Minerva appears to have been a popular choice as altars dedicated to her have been found in several places including the Roman fort of Sergontium near Caernarfon in North Wales.

Lying alongside the city walls, Chester racecourse is known as the Roodee and was originally the site of the Roman Port before silt caused the port to move downstream. A stone cross inside the racetrack and near to the Grosvenor Bridge is a clue to what is believed to be the origins of the name 'Roodee' although there are several alternative theories.

The Roodee, site of the Roman port

When the river came close to the present wall and formed the original port, there was a much larger cross, similar to the Rood Cross to be found in a church, situated on a small island or eye in the river at this point. The name Roodee is believed to have been a corruption of "The Rood Cross on the Isle".

At the base of the city wall, near to the racecourse buildings, can be found a series of large stones that clearly predate the stones of the medieval city wall. These stones are larger and show the ravages of many years. They are believed to have formed part of the original Roman wharf, others can be found near to Northgate.

The importance of the Port of Chester is borne out by the fact that it has its own Admiral and for many hundreds of years its jurisdiction covered not only the upper reaches of the River Dee but also neighbouring harbours including Liverpool.

The Watergate was the entrance to the city from the waterfront and allowed the merchants to load and unload cargo during the day without threatening the security of the city during the hours of darkness or when the city was in danger.

Not far from the Watergate, a section of the wall protrudes from the line of the wall leading to what is known as 'The Water Tower'. This tower and the section of wall were constructed to protect the edge of the harbour itself. The sheer size and strength of the fortifications are a clear indication of the sense of insecurity felt not only by the Romans but also by those who inhabited the city in more recent times.

Standing on the wall near the Watergate the keen observer may look towards Stanley Place on the far side of City Wall Street and wonder why the corner house has a porch with two outer doors opposite each other. In the days before expensive, status enhancing, motor cars, the wealthy would travel in a Sedan chair carried by retainers. Protected from the weather and the filthy, unmade roads, the more comfortably off would mount the chair, which would be positioned between the doors, in comfort and privacy. The comfort of the retainers, who would be kept waiting in the open was clearly of little importance although their position, next to the road, would ensure that passers by would be suitably impressed.

Alongside the city wall lies the Chester and Ellesmere Canal, which represented a considerable step forward in the movement of cargo – as revolutionary in its day as the present motorway system. Crossing the canal is the railway and a nearby plaque recalls the rail disaster of 1847 when the viaduct, designed by Robert Stephenson in the early years of the railway, collapsed as a train was crossing, killing four people. It is very easy to forget that the technology used to develop the railway was as advanced, in its day, as that involved in space travel today. The accident resulted in design changes to future viaducts.

Near the Northgate and alongside the city wall, the canal passes beneath a slender curved bridge joining the Blue Coat Hospital and what were formerly the walls of the Northgate prison. Prisoners were kept in appalling conditions and confined in cells below ground level with no light and little ventilation. It is no surprise, then, that records show that many prisoners died from cold, disease and general ill treatment. Ironically although severe sentences were awarded for what today are very minor crimes, if crimes at all, the souls of those condemned to death were looked after extremely conscientiously. Before execution the condemned were allowed to visit the chapel in the Blue Coat Hospital. When the canal was built in 1776 there was an obvious security risk and so the bridge was built to enable those about to die to make their peace with God. The distressing purpose of the bridge resulted in its name "The Bridge of Sighs".

On 21st September 1645, King Charles 1st stood on the Phoenix Tower on the city walls and saw his defeated army returning from the

The last walk of the condemned, the Bridge of Sighs

battle of Rowton Moor a few miles from the city. This was an important battle during the civil war and a defeat which resulted in the surrender of the city the following February.

Everyday situations contained risks which today cannot even be imagined. On 5th November 1772 a puppet show was being held on one of the upper floors of a building in Watergate Street. A large number of people, especially children, were attending but on the lower floor a quantity of gunpowder, which was far more readily available than today, was stored. During the performance it is believed that an oil lamp was knocked over causing a fire which ignited the gunpowder. Twenty-three people were killed and eighty-three were injured.

On the outskirts of the city and alongside the A41 Whitchurch Road, travellers make many suggestions as to the purpose of what appears to be a large dovecote on the top of a pole beside the road. Unfortunately this is not the nest of some giant prehistoric bird but a pump and header tank built in 1900 as part of the Victorian sewage system to help to carry the sewage over a rise in the ground.

After the Roman Legions left the city, the harbour in Chester remained very important for trade with the whole of the North West of Britain and across the sea to Ireland. Later the wars against Wales

Is it a giant bird box?

ensured that Chester remained an important strategic base but as the river began to silt it became increasingly difficult for ships to reach the city adversely affecting the ability of the city to generate wealth.

The silting of the Port of Chester and the subsequent growth of the salt marsh in the estuary of the River Dee has had considerable influence on the development of the whole of the North West of England, especially Wirral and the City of Liverpool.

The River Dee winds away from Chester between man made banks before widening into the natural estuary at a point near to Queensferry. Passing the modern Deeside Industrial Park situated on the flat ground of a former aerodrome, whose name, "Sealand", is a clear statement of its position on land reclaimed from the sea, the river flows by extensive salt marshes before reaching the Irish Sea.

Until the 1740s, the river acted as the boundary with Wales, which lies to the west, and the Wirral peninsula, which lies to the east. It was at this time that the river was channelled into man made banks in an attempt to maintain the importance of Chester as a port and enable ships to reach the city.

In the short term, the "New Cut", enabled Saltney, Sandycroft, Queensferry and Connahs Quay to develop and continue the maritime tradition of the city. This improvement bought a little time but at a cost. The physical change to the flow of the river created by the construction of the cut was far longer lasting. Without the scouring effect of the currents, which previously had flowed close to the Wirral coast, the marsh increased dramatically and spelt the doom of the Wirral ports such as Neston, Parkgate and Hoylake. It also meant that a "slice" of Wales now lay on the English side of the river.

Sandycroft, which is a few miles from Queensferry, is actually in

Wales but was once part of the Port of Chester. It was here, in 1855, that a Steam Clipper, *The Royal Charter* (2719 tons), was built. Launched sideways (as the 'New Cut' was too narrow to accept a conventional launch) the ship was used on the Liverpool to Australia run. At 336ft the ship had an iron hull, boasted watertight compartments and, being fitted with three masts and a single funnel, was powered by sail and steam.

On 27th October 1859 the ship was passing Anglesey en route to Liverpool when she was hit by a terrible storm. Carrying 103 crew and 324 passengers, she was driven onto the rocks near the village of Moelfre. Many of the passengers were returning from the Australian gold fields and carried their finds on their person. Amongst the cargo was over £500,000 of gold.

Alerted by the storm, local people turned out to try to help the passengers and crew of the stricken ship, which lay close to the low cliffs found at the scene. One member of the crew risked his life to swim to the shore carrying a line enabling a rescue lift to be erected. Although the true facts will never be fully known it is believed the female passengers thought the rescue lift to be "immodest" and held back whilst the men waited for them to seek safety first. Others jumped into the sea carrying their money belts and gold. Whatever the reasons and despite courageous efforts by both crew and local people, over 400 people died that day and visitors to Moelfre can ponder the reasons whilst looking at the memorial stone erected at the scene. Many years later, another tragedy involving a locally built vessel, the submarine *Thetis*, again made Moelfre the centre of the world's attention.

Map References

Memorial Stone for the *Royal Charter:* SH 507872

Chapter Three

The West of the Wirral Peninsula and the Chester Ports

Shotwick, Burton, Denhall, Neston, Parkgate, Gayton, Heswall and Thurstaston

The Wirral peninsula is relatively unknown to many people who live in the east or centre of the county. Rich in history and beauty the peninsula can be divided into two very different parts. The west of the peninsula faces Wales and both the geographical features and the local population have a great deal in common with the people across the water. Eastern Wirral has, in recent years, become more industrial and has connections with Liverpool and what the politicians call Merseyside.

Whenever Wirral is considered, it is important to realise that, partially due to the silting of the River Dee and the erosion of the northern coast, the physical shape of the peninsula has changed considerably since the Romans left Chester.

Shotwick, situated at the end of a cul de sac leading from the A550 Birkenhead to Queensferry Road gives every appearance of having fallen asleep in the summer sunshine and having been left behind by the passage of time. Comprising a few farms, houses, a church and an old hall, there is little evidence of the important role played during the 12th century when Shotwick was the main port for Chester and a key location in the wars between England and Wales.

The narrow road leading to the village is an ancient "Saltesway", enabling Cheshire salt to be carried to Wales by way of a causeway across the sands of the River Dee. It was along this road that the English armies of Henry II in 1156 and 1165, Henry III in 1245 and King Edward 1st in 1278 all passed on their way to fight the Welsh. The conflict with the Welsh continued for many centuries leaving a legacy of moated and fortified farms and halls which can still be found in the west of the county.

Whilst awaiting the tide, the armies camped near Shotwick Castle, the remains of which, can be found half a mile to the south of the village on the Chester side of the A550 road. Today all that can be seen is a large grass covered mound. Many of the stones that comprised the castle have been used in nearby farm buildings.

Shotwick Church itself is dedicated to St Michael and is mainly 14th century but with some earlier parts. Surrounded by the graveyard and with the warm evening light on the sandstone, the church appears timeless and peaceful.

The porch partly covers a Norman doorway whilst the door itself is 15th century. The stones on the outside of the porch carry large groves, caused by archers sharpening their arrows whilst waiting their turn at archery practice in the neighbouring fields which are still known as "the Butts". The use of the church porch to provide shelter during practice was not unique to Shotwick. The Church of St Mary at Alderley carries similar if less obvious grooves.

The ancient studded door gives access to the church, which boasts a three-decker pulpit, boxed pews and an 18th century chandelier. The whole atmosphere radiates the warm presence of generations long gone and it is easy to see ghosts, sitting in the neighbouring pews, wearing mediaeval clothes.

In the corner of the graveyard and partially hidden by a bush, is a metal ring set into the stone. This is reputed to have been used to tie up boats during the morning service. The wall which marked the riverbank is now several miles from the river which lies on the Welsh side of the Deeside Industrial Estate.

Shotwick was the setting for the famous poem by Charles Kingsley "Mary call the cattle home".

When the church is viewed from the bridge, which lay at the start of the causeway, it can be appreciated how nature has converted the former sands into pasture. Fields and hedgerows flourish giving no indication that this was once a foreshore.

In the centre of Shotwick can be found Greyhound Farm, which was originally the Greyhound inn. Used on several occasions for illegal marriages in the 17th century, the service was sometimes carried out by the schoolteacher. People from other villages were married without fulfilling the residency requirements.

Breaches of church law may be viewed as serious by clerics, but crime of a much more serious nature reached the village when, in 1710, following the murder of a traveller on the nearby Chester road, three men were arrested in the inn. One of the three incriminated the other two and they were hanged at the Gibbet Mill, which still stands

Puddington village, unchanged by time

by the side of the road near the roundabout at the junction of the A5117 and A540 roads.

Shotwick Hall is a warm comfortable looking building, built in 1662 alongside a footpath to the nearby hamlet of Puddington. Puddington itself has not developed and is a pleasant little hamlet with a few houses and a hall. The old Hall was the home of the Massey family, who played a very active roll in the affairs of the county in the 13th and 14th centuries.

The family was renown for their willingness to join in fights and their ability in combat, but, unfortunately, William Massey found himself on the losing side at the battle of Preston in 1485. Escaping from the field, he rode straight home by swimming the River Mersey at Speke. Upon arrival at Puddington, his faithful horse dropped dead in the yard. It is reported that in an attempt to give himself an alibi, Massey beat up an estate worker. However, for some strange reason, this action does not appear to have endeared him to his staff and he was denounced and arrested. He froze to death in Chester prison.

Not far from Puddington lies another attractive village, Burton, with thatched roofs, timbered cottages and an interesting church. As ships found it increasingly difficult to reach Chester, the port moved to the village of Burton with the waterfront at Denhall a mile from the village.

Denhall was the site of a hospital for poor and shipwrecked sailors as far back as the 13th century. A small village, it is difficult to accept that this peaceful little place was a major port in 1299 when King Edward granted permission for a market and by the 14th century was the embarkation port for troops sailing to Ireland. A century later Burton was trading with Spain and other countries with up to ten inns recorded in the village. There are none today.

The church is dedicated to St Nicholas, patron saint of sailors, reflecting the nautical connections of the village, whilst the clock demonstrates the changing importance of time over the years. With only one finger the clock is symbolic of a time when the passing of the minutes was of far less importance than today.

Within the graveyard are the last resting places of two priests who were martyred for their faith. Outside, by the footpath, lie the graves of two Quakers, who, in 1663, were reportedly buried standing up under the path so that the faithful could tread on their heads even in death. "The good old days?"

One of the most venerable residents of the village was Thomas Wilson, the Bishop of Sodor and Man. He was born in the village in 1663, became a bishop at the age of 34 and held the post until he died aged 93 years having refused several more rewarding posts. His cottage is situated on the main road.

Bishop Wilson's cottage, Burton

Many serious diseases have today either been eliminated or are easily treated. Clean water is expected everywhere but in the past could not be taken for granted. Alongside the road between the village and Denhall lies Hampstons Well, which served the village for centuries. All residents were expected to assist in keeping the water supply clean and heavy fines were imposed for those failing to maintain the well.

The Church at Lichfield held the manor of Burton for over 750 years. In the 19th century, the Congreave family bought the manor and held the estate until early in the 20th century. Two members of the family had the distinction of winning the Victoria Cross. They sold the manor to the son of William Gladstone the Prime Minister.

By the end of the 16th century the golden days of Burton as a port were over and the sea front at Denhall slept until 1760 when a quay was built to ship coal from a mine which worked the coal seams lying under the river.

The mine was far from ideal with very wet conditions being accounted. Coal from the face was brought to the shaft by boats propelled along tunnels by miners lying on their backs "walking" the roof. With the closure of the mine, the harbour, defeated by time and the encroaching marsh also passed into history. Today the old sea front is a haven for wildlife and a place of great beauty and solitude.

A clump of trees overlooking the front is the site of a fortification dating from the civil war. A mass grave, found at the spot, was believed to contain the bodies of passengers and crew from a ship lost in a storm whilst making the journey from Ireland.

As the salt marsh began to close around Burton, the port moved again to Neston with a new quay being constructed to assist in the movement of goods. The construction of the new quay was the subject of considerable disagreement over costing. Work started in 1541 and had not been completed thirty years later. Some of the larger ships would avoid entering the Dee estuary and lie instead at Hoyle Bank (Hoylake), at the end of the peninsula. This enabled them to avoid the difficult task of sailing up the river, which required both favourable winds and tide.

Between Burton and Neston lies Ness Botanical Gardens. Enjoying views across the estuary the garden is not only a delight to all garden lovers but also of major importance. The garden was given to Liverpool University by the family of Arthur Bulley, a successful cotton merchant, who collected rare plants from all over the world.

Passing Ness Gardens the visitor soon finds the road becoming very narrow and twisty as Ness signals the approach to the old town of Neston. Although small, Ness, or at least one of its inhabitants, is known by name or reputation to most people.

Many people can pass through Ness on a regular basis without realising it even exists yet this small hamlet could have drastically altered the course of world history in a blaze of scandal and social uproar. It was here, in Swan Cottage, which still stands next to the road, that Emma Lyon was born in the year 1765. Emma, the daughter of a Blacksmith who died whilst she was a child, later married Lord Hamilton and through her association with Admiral Nelson caused such scandal that there was a very real danger of the Admiral being replaced before the battle of Trafalgar. She was certainly a great beauty and achieved considerable influence and wealth. The death of Nelson exposed her to attacks by her enemies and she died penniless in Calais in 1815.

Emma, who was christened at Neston Parish Church, started life near the bottom of an extremely class conscious society before rising to the top and then returning to a life of considerable deprivation.

Neston itself was the most important town in Wirral with three coaches a week to London. The wealth of the town was initially as a result of serving the trade with Ireland and then between 1750 and 1928 a coal mine was established working the coal seams under the River Dee. As with the Denhall pit the Neston colliery was very wet with miners have to crouch in the cold water whilst working at the face. A large colony of rats added to the dubious pleasures of the work. The coal seams worked at Neston and Denhall ran under the river to Wales where the much larger collieries at the Point of Ayr Colliery and Gresford near Wrexham have only recently ceased operations.

Neston shows little trace of its mining history apart from colliery waste near the ruins of the quay and the Harp Inn, which overlooks the vast expanse of the marsh. The inn is not large but is full of photographs and memorabilia producing a genuine atmosphere which is an invigorating change from the canned "Theme" pubs where even the stains from old cigarette smoke come from a spray can. To sit in front of the inn on a clear day whilst looking across the marsh to the mountains of Wales would make any pint of beer taste better.

The quay at Neston was naturally called "The New Quay" to differentiate it from the earlier quay at Burton. Unfortunately the location of the quay was not particularly sheltered and this, coupled with the continued silting, resulted in another new quay being built at

Parkgate promenade. To the left can be seen Balcony House whilst Mostyn House is in the centre, beyond the white building renowned for its ice-cream.

Parkgate by the beginning of the 17th century. The ruins of the Neston Quay were sold in 1799 and some of the stones used at Parkgate. As Neston was already called the "New Quay", Parkgate became "The Old Quay" despite having been constructed more recently. Such are the quirks of life!

The harbour at Parkgate is much more obvious than at Neston or Burton. With an extensive sea wall encouraging even the less active to take a 'promenade' whilst enjoying the sea breeze and views of the Welsh mountains, the atmosphere seems to hark back to the time before the First World War. One almost expects to see ladies dressed in Edwardian bathing robes taking to the water. The sea front is lined by a variety of buildings, reflecting changing architectural styles and displaying ample evidence of the nautical past. Large houses stand next to cottages, which for centuries provided homes for the many fishermen who lived and worked the estuary.

On a summer weekend, Parkgate becomes the host to many visitors who flock to sample the local ice cream and enjoy the view. Several times a year, at high tide, the water still reaches the sea wall and the crowds multiply to several thousand. On such occasions the advancing sea water flushes out a positive feast for the many birds which feed off the estuary. In their turn, the variety and magnitude of the flocks of birds attract bird watchers, who travel for considerable distances to enjoy the benefit of the tide.

Locally caught shrimps can still be bought on the sea front, providing a reminder of the time not long ago when shrimp fishing was a major local industry until the marsh drove the fishermen further down river.

The central slip lies beside the road and opposite the Customs and Excise watch tower which protrudes into the road reducing traffic to single file ensuring visiting motor cars enter the front at a suitable speed. The slip was still used until the 1950s and for many years afterwards the hulls of several beached fishing boats lay on the mud banks.

The southern end of the promenade features the distinguished black-and-white buildings of Mostyn House School. Formerly the George Hotel and then the Mostyn Hotel, the school was founded in 1862 by the Grenfell family of Parkgate and features a clarion of 37 bells in memory of boys lost during the First World War. Many of the older readers will remember the stories of Grenfell of Labrador, the Doctor who dedicated his life to helping the Eskimo people. Wilfred Grenfell was born in the school on 28th February 1865 and grew up in Parkgate.

The Old Quay Public House stands at the end of the seafront, although a modern building replaces a much earlier inn, which provided accommodation for many travellers who waited here for passage to Ireland. The position of Parkgate, which is on a tidal river some distance from the open sea, meant that travellers might have a considerable time to explore the vicinity whilst waiting for both wind and tide to be favourable.

Amongst those recorded as staying in Parkgate is John Wesley, who visited Parkgate on many occasions during his travels. Oliver Cromwell, who was, perhaps, a less pleasant visitor and in 1741, Handel whilst en route to Dublin for the debut of "The Messiah". Not wishing to waste his time in Parkgate, Handel used the services of the choir at Chester Cathedral to complete the final touches to his great work. Due to perverse winds he eventually sailed from Holyhead but returned via Parkgate.

Opposite The 'Old Quay' are two cottages, one white, the other brown. The brown cottage was the lodgings of Emma Lyon who stayed to bathe in the sea water to cure a skin complaint. Bathing in the sea was a common treatment for skin disorders and there were several bathing machines at Parkgate. Drawn by a horse, these machines, essentially wheeled cabins, enabled ladies to take to the water in complete privacy. The white cottage has "NELSON" set in stones by the front door. Unfortunately this had nothing to do with the Admiral but remembers Nelson Burt, the son of the owner, who was drowned in a boating accident on the River Mersey in 1822.

The wide panorama of the river and estuary enables visitors to see adverse weather approaching in time to take cover in a number of welcoming tea shops until the squall has passed. A full sunset across the river with Wales caught between the water and the sky can take the breath away.

Seamen's cottages line the sea front and it is recorded that one lady drowned in her bed during a high tide. Balcony House, with its distinctive metal work edging the balconies that gave the house its name, was originally an assembly room.

The last passenger ship from Ireland to Parkgate was recorded in 1811 although a ferry service continued to operate to Flint and Bagillt across the estuary in Wales until 1850. An old inn, the Pengwern Arms, used to stand alongside the ferry terminal but has now been replaced by a restaurant called 'The Boathouse'. It is difficult to fully understand the relevance of the name until the restaurant is viewed from the air. From that position it is clear that the building was either constructed or altered to represent a ship. It may be that a previous owner had hopes of attracting those who were wealthy enough to afford their own aeroplane.

The sea wall continues from Parkgate towards the mouth of the estuary. Today the marsh has grown close to the wall and is dry apart from the occasional high tide.

The old outdoor swimming path is now a car park and the wall itself acts as a footpath for visitors walking towards Gayton. With the estuary on one side and the green of the golf links on the other, the walk, although not far, proves extremely popular especially on a fine cold day immediately after Christmas meals. Between Parkgate and Gayton is a slipway between the shore and the fields. As the water level became lower, the cattle boats from Ireland could no longer reach Parkgate and their cargo of animals was pushed overboard at this point to swim ashore by the slip.

Gayton, situated on the seaward side of Parkgate, never fully developed as a port although until the early 19th century it operated a ferry to Wales. It is believed that the service had carried travellers for more than 600 years and numbered King Edward 1st amongst its customers. He had sailed from here during one of his expeditions into Wales in 1277.

Gayton foreshore was the location for the annual "Wakes" which for many years provided an annual opportunity for people to meet and enjoy themselves with travelling entertainers. The Wakes attracted people from both sides of the river and will have acted as both recreation and the chance to carry out business.

The river front at Gayton is now almost overcome by the growth of the marsh, but the relatively deep water channel which, until the 1950s, allowed the shrimp boats to approach Parkgate, can still be seen. I remember swimming from the sea shore as a young boy.

Gayton played its part in history when, in 1690, Prince William of Orange stayed at Gayton Hall whilst en route to Hoylake from where he sailed to Ireland for the Battle of the Boyne. His host William Glegg must have provided satisfactory lodgings as he was knighted the next morning. Had King James won the battle the knighthood may have proved a mixed blessing.

It is reputed that before leaving the Prince had his horse shod by the local Blacksmith.

Gayton Mill is one of the oldest tower mills in Wirral having been built in 1735 and in use until 1875. Recently renovated, the mill stands close to the main Chester Road, where, despite its size it blends into the surroundings and can easily be overlooked.

Within a few hundred yards of the mill stand two notable buildings, which cannot fail to leave an impression on the traveller. A restaurant, "The Devon Doorway" stands alongside the roundabout at the point where the Hoylake and Brimstage roads meet. With its thatched roof and black-and-white walls, the restaurant gives the impression of great age but was, in fact, built in the 1930s.

On the Chester side of the roundabout stands the dignified shape of the Glegg Arms complete with gargoyles gazing forth from the roof. An old coaching inn, the Glegg Arms, with the name reflecting the connections with the Glegg family of Gayton Hall, has stood for many years providing refreshments and lodgings for travellers on the Chester road.

Gayton now merges with Heswall, where I grew up, and which has seen vast changes with the cosy village I once knew having grown to a small town.

To the visitor, Heswall stretches from the banks of the River Dee to the boundary with Pensby on the Birkenhead road. In fact there are two separate settlements. The main part of the village is situated on the Chester Road and is really Heswall cum Oldfield. The original village is now referred to as "Lower Village" and occupies the land below the ridge. Walking between the upper and lower villages provides wonderful views and helps to provide valuable exercise. Within the boundaries of the enlarged Heswall are areas of great natural beauty providing an opportunity for all ages to walk through the heather and gorse whilst enjoying the fresh air. The Beacons, Dales and Dungeons are like pearls on a chain. Within walking distance of each other, they, coupled with the shoreline, give access to miles of first class walks with varying levels of difficulty.

St Peter's Parish Church, built in the local sandstone, was largely rebuilt after being hit by lightning in the 19th century. The storm killed the organist and his assistant whilst causing extensive damage to the building.

It was in St Peter's that Marion and I were married in 1968, causing neither death nor damage. Despite both incidents the tower has survived since the 14th century.

The view from the church encompasses the true beauty of the peninsula. The river estuary, with its marsh merging into the water of the river, is backed by the coast of Wales and complemented by breathtaking sunsets and clean fresh air which has blown from across the Irish sea.

Overlooking the estuary is one of the finest war memorials I know. Standing between the upper and lower villages, the memorial has a view across the river to Wales which would have been familiar to all those who are commemorated on the stone.

Many of the older houses lying between the upper and lower villages reflect the success of nearby Liverpool. Large and individually designed, they contrast with the more modern developments, which are the product of present-day housing needs. Heswall has changed considerably from a county village to a small town largely acting as a dormitory for the more industrial areas of Merseyside. To me, despite the changes, Heswall will always remain a village and a wonderful place to live.

Heswall today marks the point where the marsh meets the more open water of the river. For centuries the shore was the home to fishermen who made their living from the waters of the estuary. Fishing boats still lie by the channels of deeper water in much the same way as they did at Parkgate, Neston and Shotwick but the water is more shallow every year and the grass of the marsh extends that little bit further towards the open sea. For the visitor the atmosphere can be electric as the quality of light found only on a large estuary, is joined by the sound of sea birds feeding at the edge of the marsh. In the midst of winter, a sunny day with a blue sky and a scattering of snow is a certain cure for any outbreak of winter blues.

The Welsh coast lies to the west across the water. At sunset the whole estuary is transformed into a magical picture of red and gold. It is perhaps at this time that the true beauty of the peninsula can be appreciated.

After the demise of Parkgate and Gayton, the Dee Port made a brief move to Thurstaston before crossing to the deeper water along the Welsh coast. A line of sandstone blocks almost submerged in the sand and washed by the tide are almost the only indication of the Quay at Dawpool which was almost the last attempt to retain the port of Chester on the English side of the river. The harbour was never fully developed as the estimated costs exceeded the realistic returns. The relentless advance of the marsh, aided by the decision to channel the river between Chester and Sealand in 1740 had finally put an end to any practical port facilities on the West Coast of Wirral.

The nature of the River Dee, with its tidal flow, extensive sand banks and later the creeping marsh, always made it difficult for sailing ships who depended on a favourable wind. Handel, John Wesley and others were held for weeks awaiting a favourable wind and tide. Such problems were bound to encourage competition and the more easily accessible River Mersey spawned the obvious challenger.

It is highly probable that, even without the marsh, Liverpool, which had been growing slowly between the 13th and 17th centuries, would have soon overtaken Chester. The developing Lancashire textile industry increased the importance of Liverpool, which provided a means of access to overseas markets without resorting to the atrocious road conditions existing at that time.

The opening of the first dock in 1715 together with the growth of the slave trade and the development of the triangular trade heralded a period of spectacular growth for Liverpool. Textiles from the Lancashire Mills were carried to Africa where they were exchanged for slaves. These poor unfortunate people were conveyed to the West Indies where they were sold to work on the plantations. Sugar and cotton were then carried to Great Britain. Liverpool reached a prominent position in this trade and in the ten years between 1783 and 1793 Liverpool ships carried over 300,000 slaves. The carriage of slaves in British ships was banned in 1807.

The wealth obtained from this abominable trade established Liverpool as the second port in the country but proved the final nail in the coffin for Chester.

Chester did not surrender its position to Liverpool without a fight. As late as 1825 and again in 1828, Thomas Telford, one of the most prominent engineers of his day, was approached to explore two possible alternatives to the development of Liverpool.

The first proposition was to dig a canal between Thurstaston and Birkenhead pool, which lies on the eastern side of the peninsula to provide access to the Mersey. The second, more radical idea, envisaged the construction of a floating landing stage seven miles in length between Hilbre Island and what is now the Pier Head at Liverpool. Neither idea was progressed beyond the initial stages.

It is very easy now to think both ideas ridiculous but the services of such engineers as Telford, Stephenson and Nimmo did not come cheap; nor were the merchants of Chester likely to waste money on pipe dreams.

It is perhaps worth considering that if Chester had been able to retain its lead over Liverpool then the Wirral peninsula may have developed the industries and population that now are to be found on the East bank of the River Mersey. Had this occurred, the view from Heswall across to Wales would have been somewhat different.

Map References.

Shotwick Castle: SJ 349704

Gibbet Mill: SJ 363724

Hampstons Well: SJ 308743

Ness Gardens: SJ 306753

Swan Cottage: SJ 302762

Harp Inn: SJ 289762

Chapter Four

The Wirral Coast and Islands

Irby, Thurstaston, Greasby, Caldy, West Kirby, The Hilbre Islands, Hoylake and Meols, Leasowe and New Brighton

Between Heswall and Thurstaston, but slightly inland, lies the village of Irby which, despite considerable expansion in recent years, still retains a vestige of its old atmosphere. The imposing Hall stands beside the main road surrounded on three sides by traces of the moat and defensive wall, which protected its predecessor against intrusions by the Welsh. The frontage was renovated during the 19th century.

The names of Thurstaston, which is believed to have derived from Thor, the god of war and Irby, indicate the influence of Irish-Norse Viking settlers from the eight and ninth centuries. Fresh invaders in the form of the Normans arrived in the 11th century and, after William seized power at the Battle of Hastings, the North rose in revolt. The resistance was crushed by the application of very strong repressive measures leaving much of the North as waste. Having gained control of the country William took steps to ensure that he kept his position.

In 1070 Hugh Lupus, nephew to William the Conqueror, was appointed the first Earl of Chester. Ruling from Rhuddlan and controlling a county extending to the River Ribble, Hugh Lupos needed to exercise a very firm hand to keep control. To achieve this he appointed allies to positions of power in order to manage the population. A cousin, Robert de Rodelent, was given Heswall and Thurstaston. It was probably Robert who built the first church at Thurstaston in about 1125. This building lasted until 1824 when a new building was erected. For some reason the second church only lasted until 1886 when the present structure, complete with steeple, was built. The tower of its predecessor still stands in the grounds.

Thurstaston Hall, built in the 14th century is situated next to the church and gives the impression of having windows in the loft however this is misleading as the windows are merely decoration and provide no light. As with all respectable old buildings the Hall is haunted by the ghost of a previous owner who is reported to have gained possession by disposing of the rightful heir.

Thurstaston Hill is an environmental site of special scientific interest and the location of a large red sandstone rock known as Thor's stone.

The village itself was the home to Thomas Ismay, owner of the White Star shipping line which owned several large passenger ships including the ill fated *Titanic*. Ismay bought a large house "Dawpool" in 1882 but then had it largely knocked down and rebuilt. Although the new house was demolished in 1927 the crest can still be seen on the gates which flank what was the main road from West Kirby to Heswall. A new cutting was built through the sandstone of Thurstaston Hill to keep the traffic further away from the house and to enable the old road to be incorporated into the estate. The diversion of the road also reduced the disturbance caused to the family.

Thomas Ismay was a director of the London and North West Railway Company and was instrumental in ensuring that the village railway station was built near the shore, well away from the house.

The road to the river passes the old school, now a private house, before reaching the Wirral Country Park Centre on the site of the old railway line. The centre is a fine example of the imaginative use of a former station and a neighbouring military camp.

A broad expanse of grass is ideal for children to run off steam whilst the cliff edge overlooks a wide stretch of sand which, at low tide, extends for miles towards Wales. At certain times of the year huge flocks of birds can be seen feeding in the shallow waters or rising like smoke into the sky.

The centre adjoins both the Wirral Way, which is a linear path, following the old railway line, and the shore line which carries many walkers. The buildings themselves contain a bird hide, which has always enjoyed the attention of the abundant wild life found in the area. A fine selection of walks and assisted visits to places of interest are available with information and assistance readily provided by the Rangers. Their enthusiasm is most refreshing.

Access to the sands is gained by means of a steep path, which emerges close to two old white cottages. Known as "Shore Cottages" these were originally built for two Officers of the Customs and Excise who would monitor the traffic into the ports of the river. The only access to the cottages is along the shore itself. Half buried on Thurstaston sands can be found a number of large sandstone blocks, which are all that is left of the quay at Dawpool.

From Thurstaston Hill the land drops to the rugby fields where many pupils of Calday Grange Grammar School, including myself, played and spilt blood and sweat.

On the far side of the Rugby grounds can be found a splendid black-and-white house named "Hill Bark". Part of the design is based on Little Moreton Hall near Congleton. Now a restaurant, the house has a fascinating history having been built in 1891 several miles away at Bidston, overlooking the River Mersey. As Liverpool grew and the desirability of the Mersey view decreased, the house was purchased by Sir Ernest Royden who, in 1929 had the house dismantled and then reassembled on its present site. Amongst many who have admired the house over the years was the German Crown Prince who, in 1911, had a copy erected at Potsdam. He called the house "Cecilianhof" in honour of his wife Cecilia. The house can undoubtedly claim to be an up-market mobile home with Royal connections!

Close to Hill Bark is the village of Greasby. In the centre of the village is a reproduction 18th-century Hiring Cross used as a meeting place for farmers to hire seasonal labour for work in the nearby fields.

The Mariners Column

Between the rugby grounds and West Kirby the land rises to the gorse and heather covered Caldy Hill with a stunning outlook across the roof tops of West Kirby to Wales and as far as Anglesey. At the northern end of the hill is a 60ft sandstone column with a ball at the peak. Few visitors realise the purpose of what is known as "The Mariners Column". Before 1839 a mill on the same site provided the navigators of ships bound for ports in the River Dee with a valuable navigational aid. A storm in that year destroyed the mill and it was not until 1841 that the column was erected to ensure that ships could safely negotiate the dangerous waters close to the Wirral coast. Records show that during the preparation of the foundations for the column, evidence of a chamber or tomb dating back to the Neolithic or Bronze Ages was found. Unfortunately the remains appear to have been lost or destroyed and few details are available.

Although the name of the village is spelt Caldy, the local school is Calday Grange Grammar School with the extra letter. An old school founded by William Glegg in 1636, the spelling is believed to be that in common use at that period and not a reflection of the ability of its pupils. The school had the honour to welcome me as one of its less notable scholars during my younger days. As my inability to spell is exceeded only by my abysmal writing I hold the school responsible!

In 1832 the estate of Caldy was described as being very poor, unhealthy and a most undesirable location, consisting of a few cottages and fishermen's huts. In that year a business man from Liverpool Mr R.W. Barton purchased the entire estate for £18 900. Today, the village, with its sandstone walls and pleasing vistas is a fitting tribute to the foresight and planning of Mr Barton. Caldy is one of the most desirable locations on the peninsula.

West Kirby is believed to have its origins before the Norman Conquest with its name suggesting Viking influence. A grave cover from that period shows that at least one visitor from that time remained for ever. The old part of the town lies beneath Caldy Hill with the "Ring O Bells" public house, dating back to 1806, facing the thatched roof of "The Nook", an ancient cottage, across the old main road.

The major part of the present town lies alongside the River Dee with a large marine lake providing a constant display of water sports and an invigorating walk along the surrounding wall. Enlarged some years ago, the lake is a magnet for sailing dinghies, canoes and wind surfers. Remarkable speeds are achieved by the more accomplished surfer, with the bright colours of the sails brightening all but the most miserable of days. An extensive stretch of sand has provided entertainment for many generations of children with ice cream and donkey rides available on summer weekends.

Overlooking the town is Grange Hill on which stands an imposing War Memorial dedicated in 1922 and designed by Charles Sergeant Jagger whose other works included the Royal Artillery Memorial at Hyde Park Corner.

On a bright summer day a constant stream of visitors can be seen walking the sands to the Hilbre Islands whilst others take advantage of a ride in a horse drawn cart. The multitude of visitors who find their way across the sands are not the first to visit the islands. Some 200 million years ago a Dinosaur with the unpronounceable name of Chirotherium left footprints in the sand which later formed into the

Hilbre Island and Middle Eye, with Dobbin the transport manager

rocks which make up the island. Similar footprints have been found at Thurstaston and in 1838 others were found in a Quarry at Storeton.

There are three islands making up the Hilbre Islands, Little Eye, Middle Eye, and Hilbre island itself. Their combined area amounts to about 11.5 acres and they lie in the mouth of the estuary where the River Dee meets the Irish Sea. The nearest point of the island is about one mile from the mainland.

All the islands show signs of the serious erosion which make it difficult to estimate the changing size of the islands but maps dating from the 16th and 17th centuries show a single island much larger than all three existing today. When, during the reign of Queen Elizabeth 1st, the main point of embarkation for Ireland was from the Hoyle Lake, over 4,000 troops were waiting on the islands for favourable winds and tide.

The islands form a bird sanctuary, and many varieties of birds visit the estuary. Seals can be found cavorting off the old lifeboat station at the northern end of the island or lying on the sand banks near the water, their "song" sounding eerily across the estuary.

Dolphins and porpoise have occasionally been reported near the islands although often a carcass washed up on the sand is the only indication of their presence.

On Little Eye can be found the base of an old column which when aligned with the column on Caldy Hill provided the precise fix required by marine navigators.

There is evidence of a Neolithic or Bronze Age settlement on the island and it is known that there were some inhabitants, including monks, on the islands before 1066. The head of a Norse Cross from the 10th or 11th century has been found on the island and also some old graves, for which no firm dates have been established.

The Hilbre islands were in the possession of St Werburgh's Abbey, Chester after the Norman Conquest and housed a small cell of monks. The islands were the object of pilgrimage for several centuries with groups of travellers making their way across the sands in much the same way as today's visitors. After the Abbey was dissolved in 1541 control of the islands was granted to the Dean and Chapter of Chester Cathedral before passing into the possession of a number of owners. The Liverpool Docks Trustees rented the islands from the Church and then, in 1856, the islands were bought by the Liverpool Mersey Docks and Harbour Board.

After the Second World War the islands were sold to Hoylake Urban District Council. Hilbre island itself still has the old Telegraph building which formed part of an important communications system set up to join Anglesey with the port of Liverpool.

Telegraph stations were set up at Port Lynas, Anglesey, Puffin Island, Llandudno, Llyfaen, Llanasa, Hilbre and Bidston. The stations originally used mechanical arms to pass messages by semaphore and after 1828, by telegraph.

The Telegraph provided a fast service which was also efficient, providing weather conditions permitted. One test passed a question from Liverpool to Anglesey and succeeded in receiving a reply in 23 seconds. It is also recorded that a clerk at Anglesey transmitted a rather rude comment to Liverpool when requested to repeat the answer to a question. A very short time later, the unfortunate clerk was able to read the reply informing him that he was sacked!

A large cave on the seaward side of Hilbre is known as the Lady's Cave. The story is that the daughter of the Custodian of Shotwick Castle fell in love with a young man who did not meet the approval of her father who had arranged for her to marry a Welsh Chieftain. Forcing her onto a ship en route to the wedding the father told her that her lover was dead. The maiden swooned and fell overboard to be washed ashore in the cave where she lived only long enough to tell her tale to one of the monks. The cave is named in her memory.

The ruined Lifeboat Station at the northern end of the island was managed by the Trustees of the Liverpool Docks until 1894 when the service was taken over by the Royal Lifeboat Institution, the station was closed in 1939.

The close proximity of the islands to the mainland can produce a false sense of security and conceal considerable danger. In 1842 the wife of Keeper Thomas Hughes drowned when she became lost in a blizzard whilst crossing to the island and left the safe route. The incoming tide moves very quickly and the unwary can soon be cut off from safety. The nearest point to the islands is known as Red Rocks, providing an ideal point from which to view the islands. It is not possible to cross the short distance to the island due to quicksand and adverse currents.

An ancient tale recalls how in the 12th century, Richard, Earl of Chester, was making a pilgrimage to Holywell in Flintshire when he has ambushed by hostile Welsh forces. His call for assistance was answered by his Constable who rode with a relief force to Hilbre expecting to find sufficient ships to sail, with his men, across to the Welsh coast. Upon reaching Hilbre he discovered there were no ships present. Knowing his Lord was in danger he sought the aid of the monks and through the power of prayer the waters parted allowing him to pass and rescue the Earl. The monks are now long gone and all those who wish to cross the sands should follow the more mundane but more reliable designated route.

At Red Rocks can be found old coast guard houses and a now redundant lighthouse. For many older people, Red Rocks was the special place were families would picnic whilst the younger children built sand castles. Golfing enthusiasts hold the neighbouring Royal Liverpool Golf Club in great regard and local sand dunes are home to the natterjack toad and other endangered species.

At the West Kirby end of Hoylake promenade is a road named "Kings Gap" after the day in 1690 when Prince William of Orange, having stayed the previous night at Gayton, joined his ships at the Hoyle Lake in order to travel to Ireland and his meeting with King James on the banks of the River Boyne. The army was camped at Hoylake and on Hilbre Island before they embarked. The Hoyle Lake was part of the port of Chester and for many years provided a deep water facility which avoided the problems of entering the Dee.

On a side road off Kings Gap and several hundred yards from the shore stands the one remaining Hoylake lighthouse. Now a private dwelling, the building towers above the surrounding houses but blends in so well with its surroundings that it is easy to miss. As the coast line altered and the Hoyle Lake silted, the importance of

Hoylake declined until today almost the only reminder is the name "Kings Gap".

Alongside Hoylake lies Meols with wide stretches of sand providing space for all manner of seaside activities. Fishing boats operate from the foreshore and the sand gives ample opportunity for horse riders to exercise their mounts to the maximum. There are views of shipping entering the River Mersey, whilst Southport and Blackpool can be clearly seen. On a very fine day the hills of the Lake District can be picked out especially when their slopes are covered in snow.

Hoylake lighthouse, standing some way from the sea

The shape of this section of coast has changed considerably over the centuries. The substantial sea defences, which stretch from Meols to New Brighton, are all that prevent serious inroads by the waves. Although far from attractive it is only the sea wall that has enabled development to take place at Moreton and Leasowe.

Beneath the sands lie a submerged forest and a Roman settlement long lost to the sea. It is believed that the Romans built a road leading from Chester to Meols although its course has never been properly established. Many artefacts have been found in or near the old forest including Greek and Roman coins as well as Saxon items. Very little pottery has been found which could be an indication of an embarkation port rather than a fixed settlement.

A brisk walk along the sea defences soon brings sight of Leasowe Lighthouse. A continuing process of renovation is in progress and the lighthouse is often open to the public. The number of marine navigational aids found along the northern coast of Wirral is indicative of the many dangers facing shipping approaching the ports of Chester and Liverpool in the days before steam and modern radar.

The Mariners Column at Caldy together with the alignment column on the Hilbre Islands assisted ships sailing into the Dee. A pair of lighthouses was sited at both Hoylake and Leasowe. Lighthouses were normally built in pairs so a navigator could establish precise positions by obtaining a fix on two known lights. In the case of the lighthouses at Hoylake and Leasowe both pairs of lights had an upper and a lower light. Once the upper light was directly above the lower light then an accurate bearing could be obtained. The Hoylake and Leasowe lights were Leading Lights, emitting a steady beam intended to lead vessels into a safe channel or anchorage. The Hoylake lights were intended to lead vessels into the Hoyle Lake which served Chester, whilst the Leasowe lights guided ships along the Horse and Rock channels which passed close to the Wirral coast en route to Liverpool. The lower light at Hoylake has long been removed but was situated near the lifeboat station. The remaining lighthouse was the upper light.

Permission to erect the Leasowe light was granted in 1761 and by 1763 two lights were completed. The existing one was originally the upper light whilst a lower light was erected on the shore line. Always an exposed and windswept coast, the sea later claimed the lower light, which was destroyed in a storm. Rather than build a new light in such an inhospitable place, a new upper light on Bidston Hill was opened in 1873 with the Leasowe light becoming the lower light.

The approach along the Horse and Rock channels was helped further by a light on Whelford Hill at the Point of Ayr on the Welsh side of the River Dee and by a further lighthouse at the mouth of the River Mersey at New Brighton.

The Perch Rock Lighthouse was built on a dangerous rock known as Black Rock but took its name from an earlier wooden construction in which the warning lamp resembled a bird's perch. The light was switched on in 1830.

In July 1908 all the Wirral lights were switched off for the last time. A decision had been made to change the main channel for shipping approaching Liverpool from the Horse and Rock channels to the more easily maintained Crosby channel, which followed the Lancashire side of the estuary. The guiding tasks of the lighthouses were taken over by a line of buoys backed up by lightships which were themselves later replaced.

Despite the pleasing aspect of the Wirral coast, the dangers to shipping meant that, until the middle of the 19th century, the population of North Wirral enjoyed a reputation of being second only to the Cornish for using merchandise obtained from wrecks as an illicit source of income. There was, however, no suggestion that they ever deliberately wrecked ships passing the coast.

Near the Leasowe Lighthouse is the strange looking building of

Leasowe Castle built in 1593 by the 5th Duke of Derby. Now a hotel, the building was originally a fortified house, built to provide protection in a very wild and lawless area. By the end of the 17th century the house was in a poor state reflected by the name "Mockbeggar Hall" which was a common name for a deserted building. Sir Edward Cuss took over the building in 1826 and made it the family home. Panelling in the dinning room is reputed to be from the original Star Chamber in Westminster although I know of at least one other claimant for the honour. From 1910 until 1970 the building was used as a home for retired railway workers apart from a period in the Great War when it accommodated German prisoners of war.

Until a few decades ago a wooden seat could be found by the sea wall carrying a carved inscription " Sea come not hither nor wet the sole of my foot". The seat is regarded, locally, as positive proof that this was the spot where King Canute defied the waves. The alternative suggestion that the seat had been carved on the instructions of Sir Edward Cuss is disregarded. After the Second World War the seat fell into disrepair and finally disappeared. Although a number of other locations claim to have been the site of the King's confrontation with the waves, few, if any, offer such positive proof.

It was from the sea wall near Leasowe Castle that the world's first passenger carrying Hovercraft service began. The Vickers VA3 was introduced between Moreton and Holyhead on 20th July 1962 by British United Airways and remained in service until September 14th of the same year when it was damaged by heavy seas and withdrawn. Although the first craft was extremely small, the idea has progressed to the huge crafts to be found crossing the English Channel every day.

New Brighton at the mouth of the River Mersey was the location of a tower higher than that across the water at Blackpool. The tower, 621 feet high, was demolished soon after the Great War but the supporting building remained in use as a ballroom until a fire in 1969. Tower Gardens at the base of the tower was filled with an extensive outdoor funfair including a "Wall of Death", where motor cycles raced around a vertical cylinder, "The Fly" where visitors were stuck against the wall of a rotating cylinder whilst the floor fell away and many other more common attractions including a miniature railway. Visitors from Liverpool would travel by ferry boat to the New Brighton pier, filling the town to capacity and beyond on a sunny weekend.

Although the tower, outdoor funfair, ferry boat and pier have long gone the town still possesses an indoor fair in a wonderful art deco

The indoor Funfair, New Brighton

building next to the sea front. After a period of decline the town has been much improved in recent years.

Fort Perch Rock, built in 1897 to defend the river stands next to the lighthouse whilst a model boating lake on the promenade is a "must" for those with children or who enjoy people-watching. On a sunny day a selection of model ships can be found being displayed by enthusiasts keen to show their pride and joys to interested watchers.

I have seen several notable characters, including an Admiral in full uniform from the waist up and jeans and trainers below. The models demonstrate the skills and enthusiasm of their makers and at times include such gems as radio controlled rubber rings and model ducks.

Map References

Thors Stone: SJ 245847

Hill Bark: SJ 244858

Mariner's Column: SJ 224866

Telegraph Building, Hilbre: SJ 185881

Leasowe Lighthouse: SJ 252913

Chapter Five

Maritime Cheshire

Bidston, Liscard, Birkenhead, Tranmere, Rock Ferry, Thornton Hough, Brimstage, Eastham, Willaston and Ellesmere Port

It is only a few miles along the River Mersey from Wallasey to New Ferry yet this stretch is rich in maritime history.A broad promenade runs alongside the river from the site of the New Brighton tower for about two miles to the landing stage at Seacombe. Ferry boats operate a triangular service from Seacombe to the Woodside terminal in Birkenhead and then across the river to Liverpool. On a sunny day this is a very cheap and enjoyable cruise with much to be seen on both sides of the water.

A short distance along the promenade and a little distance inland lie what remains of the Wallasey Magazine which was used from 1751 until 1851 to store the powder and shot from ships entering the river. The danger of oil lamps, wooden ships and gunpowder should be obvious but in 1763 the brig *Charlotte* caught fire and blew up before she could be unloaded causing considerable damage and death.

In January the following year the merchant ship *Lottie Sleigh* had just loaded her cargo including dynamite when she caught fire off Woodside. The crew had sufficient warning to escape but most of the windows in Birkenhead and Liverpool failed to survive the night and glaziers had to be brought into the city from the surrounding area. Little was left of the ship apart from the figurehead, which apparently survived almost intact.

Until 1751 the Liverpool Magazine was situated at the top of Brownlow Hill. Eventually someone had the sense to realise that the carriage of large quantities of gunpowder, stored in barrels, through the centre of a busy, rough city was less than desirable.

When the Wallasey magazine was built it was located in a wild desolate area of sand dunes. As Liverpool increased in importance so the magazine required workers and storage facilities. A whole com-

The Mersey ferry "Mountwood" off Seacombe terminal

munity grew up around the magazine and this became known as "Gunpowder Village".

Although most of the village has now gone, the village pub and the round house used by the watchman are still there together with the entrance gate to the Liscard Battery which was built in 1858 as a second line of defence in support of Fort Perch Rock. Despite being almost engulfed by more recent housing the magazine is still remembered by the road and pub names and acts as a reminder of the days of sail, cannon and wooden ships.

Further along the promenade and facing the river is a modern retirement home known as Mother Redcap's. Close to both Wallasey town hall and Seacombe Ferry, the home is a gentile and pleasant looking building with an information stone outside giving just a hint of a rather different past. The original establishment was a famous, or infamous, meeting place for smugglers and the many sailors who would rest between voyages in the shelter of the Wirral coast.

Governments have always been reluctant to spend money on the armed forces with the result that during the early stages of many wars the operational efficiency of the services has been seriously threatened by the parsimonious attitude of the Treasury. During the 18th century the lack of strength in the navy had created the need for Pri-

Wallasey Town Hall from the river

vateers who were in effect privately funded warships which were authorised to attack the enemies of the country.

Many Privateers operated from the Mersey in the late 18th century and legend holds that, in the days before high street banks, Mother Redcap looked after the treasures, legal and illegal, of sailors and smugglers. As many failed to return from distant voyages she was able to keep a great deal of their wealth. After her death many tried to find the hidden treasure but it has never been found. It is reputed to have been concealed in the many tunnels that are believed to run between Wallasey and New Brighton.

On Bidston Hill, which overlooks Wallasey and Birkenhead can be found a solitary windmill, complete with sails, visible from all over the peninsula and across the Mersey in Liverpool. The mill at Bidston was built to replace an earlier mill destroyed in 1791 and worked until about 1875. Traces of a still earlier peg-mill can be found alongside the present structure.

A number of rock carvings, including the outline of a horse can be found nearby. Despite some arguments, which consider the carvings to be Iron or Bronze Age, others consider the 18th century to be more probable.

Holes in the rock were used to support poles carrying the flags of shipping companies based in Liverpool. When first sighted on the approach to Anglesey, the identity of a ship would be relayed by a series of signalling stations, including the one on Hilbre Island, to Bidston, where the house flag of the ships owners would be raised to warn the docks to prepare a berth.

Close to the windmill can be found Bidston Lighthouse, built to replace the original lower Leasowe light. Alongside the lighthouse and visible for many miles are the twin domes of the Proudman Oceanographic Laboratory. Britain's oldest marine laboratory is at the forefront of research into the sea bed and the movements of the oceans. The oil and gas industry certainly value the information which flows from a building which is over 130 years old.

During the 19th century, Birkenhead, which faces Liverpool across the fast flowing River Mersey, grew from a small village to a large town tipped as a model city to be. The present day shows that the dream failed to materialise yet there are several notable achievements to record.

Birkenhead was the first town in Europe to have a public tramway, a horse drawn system opened in 1860, the first public library in the country and a public park designed by the same architect as Central Park, New York. The First World War poet Wilfred Owen attended Birkenhead Institute and it was in Birkenhead in 1908 that Baden Powell announced the launch of the Scout Movement. Nearby Arrowe Park was host to the World Scout Jamboree in 1929 which was visited by over 50,000 scouts from 60 countries.

Birkenhead Priory, site of the original "Ferry across the Mersey," dates back to the 12th century with the monks having the rights to provide the service from what was known as Monks Ferry alongside the priory. The present ferry to Liverpool operates from Woodside about half a mile from the Priory. Serving both Woodside and Seacombe the Mersey ferry boats carry commuters and visitors across to the Pier Head in Liverpool. All ferries now carry a red and black funnel but until recently there were two distinct "lines". The Birkenhead to Liverpool carried the red and black whilst the Wallasey and Seacombe boats sported black and white funnels.

Before the recent growth in privately owned motor vehicles the ferry boats provided the main means for commuters crossing the river. A regular morning entertainment was to watch the office workers perambulate around the upper deck in a never ending circle and always in the same direction.

There is an underground railway between Birkenhead and Liver-

Full-sized replica of *Resurgam*, the world's first mechanically powered submarine, at Birkenhead

pool with frequent electric trains. When the line opened in 1886 it was the longest underwater railway tunnel in the world and until 1903 used steam engines. The atmosphere, in an enclosed tunnel with restricted ventilation, must have been both unpleasant and unhealthy.

Road transport crossed the river on the ferry boats, access to which was gained by a floating roadway designed to cope with the rise and fall of the tide. The remains of the roadway can be seen alongside the Woodside Terminal and alongside the Liver Building in Liverpool.

As the use of motor vehicles increased so the problems of carrying those wishing to cross the river became more critical. The nearest point to cross the Mersey, apart from the ferry, was at Runcorn where a transporter bridge had been built in 1905 capable of carrying a limited number of vehicles and passengers across to Widnes on the northern shore.

It was obvious that a means had to be found to meet the growing needs of road transport. Consideration was given to building a bridge but this would have been vulnerable to attack in war and if damaged, might have blocked the port of Liverpool.

"Queensway", the first road tunnel under the river, opened in

1934 and for some years was the longest underwater road tunnel in the world. Several decades later, as traffic increased, a second tunnel, "Kingsway", was built to carry traffic from the M53 motorway, at Wallasey, under the river.

Whilst the construction of the tunnels and the railway made crossing the river much easier it obviously reduced the number of people using the boats and the number of ferry routes has reduced over the years.

In Birkenhead Docks can be found "The Historic Warships", a collection of ships open to the public. Two veterans of the Falklands conflict, a Frigate and a submarine, lie alongside the wharf whilst a slightly battered, but intact, German U Boat lies on the jetty.

U534 has a rich story. The only U-boat to be raised after being sunk in action, she sailed in the final days of the war on a secret mission having been loaded with a cargo of boxes brought to the boat under very heavy security. Carrying a South American radio operator and with all fuel tanks full it was believed that she was bound for South America where many top Nazis had fled. When all U Boats were ordered to surrender *U534* did not and continued her mission until, on May 5th 1945, she was caught on the surface by the RAF and attacked. Badly damaged, she remained on the surface long enough for all her crew to escape. Three men died in the water before they could be rescued but as nobody died onboard the submarine the wreck was not a war grave.

With the passing of the years the value of the treasure she carried increased attracting the attentions of speculators. In 1993 she was finally raised and carried to the shore. On examination the boxes were located and the excitement increased to a new height!. The moment eventually came and the boxes opened to reveal "German Army condoms!" It would appear that either someone was double crossed in 1945 or that somebody had devised a cunning plan!

The dock, which houses the Historic Warships, was used in 1878 for the diving trials of the world's first mechanically powered submarine *Resurgam* built alongside the dock by the Garratt Submarine Navigation Company . In recent years *Resurgam* has been located off Anglesey and it is planned to raise her before this unique vessel is lost for ever. A full size replica of *Resurgam* can be found alongside the Woodside Ferry terminal and standing on part of the old floating roadway.

Alongside Birkenhead Priory lies Cammell Laird Shipbuilders

who were responsible for many famous ships during the 19th and 20th centuries.

The Confederate commerce raider *Alabama* was built in 1862 proving extremely successful, sinking or capturing about 60 Union ships. The Union States took the view that providing a warship was a serious breach of neutrality and an enormous political scandal resulted. Britain was forced to pay compensation.

Founded in 1828 the yard once employed over 40,000 workers. Amongst the many ships built for the Royal Navy were the battleships *HMS Rodney* and *HMS Prince of Wales* which, at 35000 tons each, were amongst the largest ships in the world at the time of their launch.

Princess Mary launched *HMS Rodney* on 17th December 1925. At the first attempt the bottle of champagne failed to break. On the second attempt Her Royal Highness managed to completely miss the 35,000-ton Battleship poised a few feet away, so destroying her chances of selection for the Windsor Castle darts team!

A matter of weeks after being accepted by the navy *HMS Prince of Wales*, together with *HMS Hood* engaged the German battleship *Bismarck*. In a brief battle *HMS Hood* exploded causing a horrendous loss of life. *HMS Prince of Wales* later joined the war against the Japan but was lost together with *HMS Repulse* whilst operating without air cover in an effort to stop the advance of the Japanese Army.

Two aircraft carriers both carrying the name *HMS Ark Royal* were built at Birkenhead. The first, launched in 1937, was the first ship for the Royal Navy to be designed and built as an aircraft carrier. Other carriers of the period were initially built for other roles and then converted. The two carriers bearing the name *Ark Royal* were the third and fourth ships bearing that name to serve in the Royal Navy.

The launch of the first *Ark Royal* to be built at Birkenhead proved similar, in some respects to that of *HMS Rodney*. Lady Maude Hoare D.B.E., wife of the First Lord of the Admiralty, launched her on 13th April 1937. Unlike Princess Mary, Lady Hoare did not miss the ship entirely, but it took her four attempts before the bottle of champagne broke.

I will always remember seeing the launch of the second Birkenhead built *Ark Royal* on 3rd May 1950. I stood with my dad close to the bow of the great ship as the bottle broke and can still hear the sound of the ships' sirens welcoming her to the water. Many other warships, especially submarines, together with a considerable number of passenger ships were launched at Birkenhead including the *Mauretania, which* is still remembered with affection by many on Merseyside.

A memorial in Birkenhead Priory records a tragedy that shocked the whole country but especially the close knit society of Merseyside. In June 1939 the submarine *HMS Thetis* having been built at Cammell Laird, sailed for her diving trials in Liverpool Bay. Carrying her full complement of crew and many representatives of her builders, the submarine failed to surface after her first dive. Although there were many factors involved, the actual cause was the opening of both front and rear doors of a torpedo tube. This resulted in water flooding the two forward compartments causing the bow of the submarine to remain on the sea bed.

The newspapers carried photographs of the stern of the submarine showing above water while readers and families were assured that a safe rescue was almost a formality. Families, desperate for news and starved of information were treated very badly having to gather at the shipyard to wait for news of the rescue.

Great courage was shown by those trapped, who followed Admiralty instructions to wait for vessels to arrive on the surface before escaping. Unfortunately many of the service personnel had little or no training with the escape equipment and the workers from the shipyard and other civilian firms had received no training at all.

Due to a lack of efficient wireless the Tug accompanying the submarine had to send a telegram to Submarine Headquarters informing them that Thetis was apparently in difficulty. This message was further delayed whilst the delivery boy mended a puncture in his bicycle. Slow response by the Navy followed the realisation that the submarine was in trouble and this, together with the unusually large number of people on board, meant that the available air supplies were limited. The rescue, hampered by a lack of specialist knowledge and equipment, had to contend with adverse tide conditions. Only four men escaped from the submarine and they reached the surface through the efforts of those trapped below. Time ran out for the remaining 99 men and they perished with assistance all around but unable to help.

Many of the civilian workers and some of the naval crew came from the Merseyside area where the tragedy was deeply felt. The loss was the subject of a full enquiry but by then war had broken out and a great number of people believed that the findings were a cover up designed more to protect the Admiralty than find the true cause. More than sixty years after the disaster, many remember the loss with a mixture of sorrow and bitterness. At the time it was the world's worst submarine disaster.

The memorial to *Thetis* was unveiled at Birkenhead Priory in June 1999, sixty years after the events in Liverpool Bay. A plate showing a line drawing of the boat and the simple facts of her loss is set at the base of St Mary's Tower. There is nothing special about the memorial until a visitor climbs the steps to the top of the tower which overlooks the yard in which the submarine was built and later reborn with a different name.

On each step of the staircase, there is a simple plaque with the name of each of the 99 men who lost their lives in *Thetis*. From the Captain to the two caterers who were there to provide the celebration meal on her great day and who died in her, all are remembered.

Many of those who died in the disaster are buried in a mass grave in Holyhead, Anglesey. An imposing monument it records all who died, naval or civilian. Even on a sunny day it is impossible to look at the neat lines of names without being deeply moved and asking that old question "Why?".

It is sad to reflect that one of the naval men who survived was not paid for several months after the rescue as he was unable to produce his paybook in accordance with regulations. The book lay with the rest of the crew in the hull of the submarine.

The submarine was eventually raised and carried to the shore at Moelfre where she was beached until the remains of the crew could be recovered. Returned to the Cammell Laird yard for refitting *Thetis* was renamed *Thunderbolt* and served with distinction before taking her second crew on her final dive following a sustained depth charge attack by the Italian Navy. *Thunderbolt* is remembered on the submarine memorial at the Embankment, London.

Next to the shipyards is a short stretch of sand at Tranmere. Today, Tranmere is known mainly for its football team and oil terminal but it was here, in 1888, that one of the world's most advanced shipping experiments met her end.

The *Great Eastern*, intended to sail non-stop from Liverpool to Australia, was well ahead of her time. Originally she was intended to be called *Leviathan* but the name change occurred before the launch. Designed by Isambard Kingdom Brunel, she was, at almost 19,000 tons and displacing almost 30,000 tonnes, the largest ship in the world. With five funnels, six masts and powered by both sail and steam engines driving paddle wheels, she sailed many times from Liverpool to America. Drastically under powered and expensive she was renowned as an unlucky ship. She was built on the Thames and due to the size of the ship and the location of the yard it was planned that her launch would take several days. Sticking in her cradle and requiring far more equipment than was expected, her launch commenced on 3rd November 1857 but it was not until 31st January 1858 that she finally took to the water. One workman was killed during the launch.

On 9th September 1859 she was finally ready for her sea trials and quickly worked up to 13 knots. Unfortunately two valves on the high pressure cooling system had not been opened and the resulting explosion killed 6 men. Brunel, by this time, was a very sick man and he died a few days later on September 15th 1859.

The cost of running the ship was too high for private enterprise and she became a cable layer for several years. There was potential to use her size and fame for commercial purposes and, from 1886 until 1888, she was positioned in the River Mersey as a floating exhibition for Lewes's Stores. It was at Tranmere in 1890 that she was finally broken up. When the hull was cut open the bodies of two of the builders were found between the plates having been sealed inside since her construction. Some of her fittings were removed and used to furnish a public house, called appropriately the "Great Eastern", in neighbouring New Ferry.

Many people in Cheshire are aware of the Conway Centre situated on the Menai Straits where school children from Cheshire are able to spend a short time learning the skills of sailing in the waters of the Menai Strait.

The relationship between Conway and Cheshire is not as recent as many may believe. Three old Training Ships, the "wooden walls", *Conway*, *Indefatigable* and *Akbar*, were moored off New Ferry for almost ninety years. *Conway* was a cadet training ship for officers of the Royal and Merchant Navy whilst *Indefatigable* trained disadvantaged youngsters for a life at sea. *Akbar* served as a reformatory school.

The last Conway was a 91-gun ship of the line from Nelson's day. Built as *HMS Nile* she replaced an earlier *Conway* and had taken up position off Rock Ferry in 1876. Former pupils included Captain Webb, who became the first man to swim the Channel and the poet John Masefield.

In 1941 the *Conway* was moved to the Menai Strait where she remained until 1953 when she was lost after striking a sandbar whilst

The Lady Lever Art Gallery, Port Sunlight

en route for a refit. Her anchor cable can still be seen near to the Conway Centre awaiting her return. Visitors to the Maritime Museum in Liverpool will pass a large, old-fashioned anchor near the entrance. This was the anchor from *Conway*.

Conway remained as a shore establishment until 1974 when the Cheshire County Council took over the management of the centre. Close to the Centre a board carrying the name "Indefatigable" directs visitors to a training establishment of that name. Conway and Indefatigable are still neighbours after more than one hundred years.

The *Akbar* also left the sea and became a shore establishment at Heswall for many years before finally closing.

To those visiting for the first time, Port Sunlight is quite bewildering in its concept. The first sod for the village was turned on 3rd March 1888, yet the houses and facilities would receive universal acclaim if they were to be created today. Built by William Lever for the workers of his soap factory the estate provided everything for their needs including schools, churches and a library. The Lady Lever Art Gallery was built in 1914 as a memorial to Lady Elizabeth. At the opposite end of the long rose beds is the war memorial, itself a masterpiece of architecture, recalling the tragic losses of company employees. It reflects great credit on the company that, when the memorial was dedicated, the ceremony was performed not by those of high rank or social position but by a Sergeant and a Private, both former employees, who had suffered terribly in war.

Although now overshadowed by Port Sunlight, nearby Bromborough Pool was the home of an earlier initiative in social provision. In 1853 James Wilson established the northern branch of Prices' Patent Candle Company of Battersea. The company provided a high standard of housing and facilities for workers including schools and churches. Each day started with ten minutes of prayer, five minutes in company time and five in the employees'.

Many social climbers of the time were proud to know Mr Price and several boasted of having such a prominent associate. In truth Mr Price kept more than just a low profile, he did not exist!. The character was "invented" by William Wilson and his partner Mr Lancaster when they formed the company in 1830 and chose the name and personality of Mr Price to avoid a loss of dignity to their own names. The Company later became part of Unilever.

Next to Port Sunlight lies Cheshire's answer to Hollywood. The Oval Sports ground in Bebington was used in the film "Chariots of Fire" to act as the location for the Olympic Games. The Woodside Ferry Terminal also featured in the film as the channel port.

If Port Sunlight was the creation of Lord Leverhulme then the village of Thornton Hough, as it stands today, was largely created by two business men, Lord Leverhulme and Joseph Hirst. The village, which featured in the Domesday Book, was altered considerably, by Joseph Hirst, a Yorkshire business man, who made a number of changes in the centre of the village including building the Parish Church in 1867.

It was Lord Leverhulme however, who transformed the village to house many of his estate workers. The village reflects an earlier, perhaps imaginary period. The old Smithy lies in the shadow of the spreading Chestnut tree whilst the black-and-white cottages overlook the village green which resounds to the sound of Sunday cricket.

Thornton Hough boasts two outstanding churches. The Unitarian Church was built for the village in 1906 by Lord Leverhulme, whilst the Parish Church has two clock faces on one side. Joseph Hirst was unable to see the main face from his bedroom window in Thornton House and so installed a second, smaller face above. Although a normal household clock would have been more practical, the choice of a second face ensured a form of immortality.

From Thornton Manor, home to Lord Leverhulme since 1888, an arc of tree lined avenues radiate from the house reflecting a more

Glimmer of the past: the lighthouse, Ellesmere Port

stately time when a horse drawn carriage was the preferred means of transport.

Close to Thornton Hough lies the hamlet of Brimstage with its ancient hall which includes a fortified tower dating back at least to the 14th century when the wars with Wales were still raging. The village hall and the old school provide a tranquil setting to the hamlet where a craft centre acts as a magnet to all who enjoy embroidery and other hand crafts.

A gargoyle in Brimstage Hall is reputed to be the inspiration for the Cheshire Cat in "Alice in Wonderland", however many places make similar claims. The idea of a gargoyle acting as the inspiration for the smile on the face of the Cheshire Cat is certainly more pleasant than some theories I have come across.

Not far from Brimstage lies Willaston where the village green hosts a fine display of spring bulbs and the old railway station is the start of the Wirral Country Park. The park provides one of the most scenic walks in the county following the old railway line across the peninsula to Parkgate, Thurstaston and then West Kirby. The station was closed to rail traffic in the 1960s but is beautifully presented as if it was fully operational. Willaston Hall built in the 17th century, looks on the present village with a benevolent pleasing gaze.

From Willaston it is not far to Eastham with its old ferry terminal, woods and the entrance to the Manchester Ship Canal. Although the ferry, which used to carry workers and day trippers between Liverpool and Eastham, has long ceased to function, the jetty and the taxi rank remain.

Walking amongst the trees and listening to the birds it is difficult to believe that, until the ferry closed in 1929, the woods and surrounding fields would be full of people enjoying a break from city life.

The Ferry Hotel, which still faces the river across the broad grass lawns, used to stand alongside a Triumphal Arch similar to the *Arc de Triomphe* in Paris. The arch was the entry point to gardens, which must have been the "Alton Towers" of their day. The gardens held a funfair, which included a tubular ride enabling passengers to "loop the loop" at speeds of up to 95 mph, and a small zoo. One performer was Blondin, famous for walking a tightrope across the Niagara Falls. Today's visitors can enjoy a picnic by the banks of the river whilst watching passing ships making their way to the bar and the open sea.

Ellesmere Port lies alongside the Manchester Ship Canal and at the end of the much older Ellesmere Canal, which connects the town to what was then the industrial area of Shropshire. The town is home to the Boat Museum providing a rare opportunity to look at the history of the canals and the people who lived and worked on the narrow boats.

At the point, near the museum, where the Ellesmere Canal joins the Manchester Ship Canal, stands a small lighthouse. It is not immediately apparent why a lighthouse should be situated in this particular location as little danger could be expected at the junction of two canals. In fact the lighthouse was built in 1802 at a time when the Ellesmere Canal joined the River Mersey and not the Manchester Ship Canal which would not be constructed for over ninety years.

Between Ellesmere Port and Eastham and directly alongside the Ship Canal is a small hill named Mount Manisty. This hill was constructed from the spoil created in the construction of the canal and separates the canal from the river.

The nearby Stanlow Oil Refinery is situated on the site of an ancient Abbey. During the Second World War when the military planners were working on the plans for "D" Day, the invasion of Europe, they realised that they faced a number of very basic problems. In order to land and supply the invading armies, ports and a prodigious amount of fuel would be required. It was apparent that the German High Command would do their utmost to ensure that neither shelter nor fuel would be available to Allied forces. On 6th June 1944 the invasion finally took place with the Allies carrying with them a prefabricated harbour known as Mulberry Harbour and a pipe line which carried fuel directly from Stanlow down the length of England before crossing under the channel to France. For security reasons this pipe line under the sea was given the code name of a cartoon character "Pluto".

The small village of Capenhurst illustrates the complexities of modern Cheshire.

Modern technology in the form of an industrial site owned by British Nuclear Fuels overlooks an ancient pinfold standing by the main road in the centre of the village. The pinfold was used to pen straying sheep and cattle belonging to residents until a set release fee was paid. Other examples can be found at Bebington and at Little Budworth. In the modern day a wheel clamp carries out much the same purpose but with far less style.

Wirral is full of history. Much local in nature but some of national or even international interest. Many of the local "Oddities" may not be of earth shattering importance but they do make the peninsula a wonderful and fascinating place to live.

Across the old Ince marshes the ground rises towards Helsby Hill and its old Iron Age Fort overlooking the M56 motorway. It is now time to look at the remainder of Cheshire.

Map References

Bidston Mill: SJ 288894

Mother Redcaps: SJ 320917

Historic Warships: SJ 318903

Birkenhead Priory: SJ 328886

Price's Village: SJ 349842

Brimstage Hall: SJ 305828

Eastham Ferry: SJ 365818

Mount Manisty: SJ 391790

Capenhurst Pinfold: SJ 365738

Chapter Six

The Border with Wales

Farndon, Shocklach, Bickerton, Tushingham, Peckforton, Tarporley, Nantwich, Audlem and Combermere

To the south of Chester the county boundary initially follows the line of the River Dee. The border with Wales has changed many times over the centuries as the tides of war flowed in favour of the English or Welsh. The present border presents a very peaceful picture with small villages clustered round old churches set amidst the fields.

Farndon, which lies on the English side of the river, is joined to Holt on the Welsh side, by a 14th-century arched bridge. King Edward the Elder, King of Wessex, died here in 924 whilst involved in a bitter war with the Welsh.

Until the main Nantwich to Wrexham road was moved outside the village, traffic was heavy with continual traffic jams at the narrow bridge. At the time of the civil wars this bridge contained a drawbridge to allow more control over traffic crossing the border. Serious fighting took place here in 1643 between the Welsh who supported the King and Parliamentary forces commanded by Sir William Brereton for Parliament. The bridge was important as it lay on the main supply routes from Wales to the City of Chester, which was held by the King. Only after the drawbridge was forced by the English were the Welsh repelled.

John Speed, famous for his maps, was born here in 1552 later moving to London. He was the father of eighteen children.

Alongside the Chester road lies a memorial bearing a striking resemblance to Cleopatra's Needle which stands on the Victoria Embankment in London. Carrying the name "Barnston", the needle, with its guardian lions, commemorates Major Roger Barnston, who died of wounds on 23rd December 1857 during the relief of Lucknow.

A few miles south of Farndon, and close to the Welsh border, lies the small hamlet of Shocklach. Only those who are determined will find the tiny 12th-century church, which stands amidst the fields some distance from the village. The search is well worth the effort

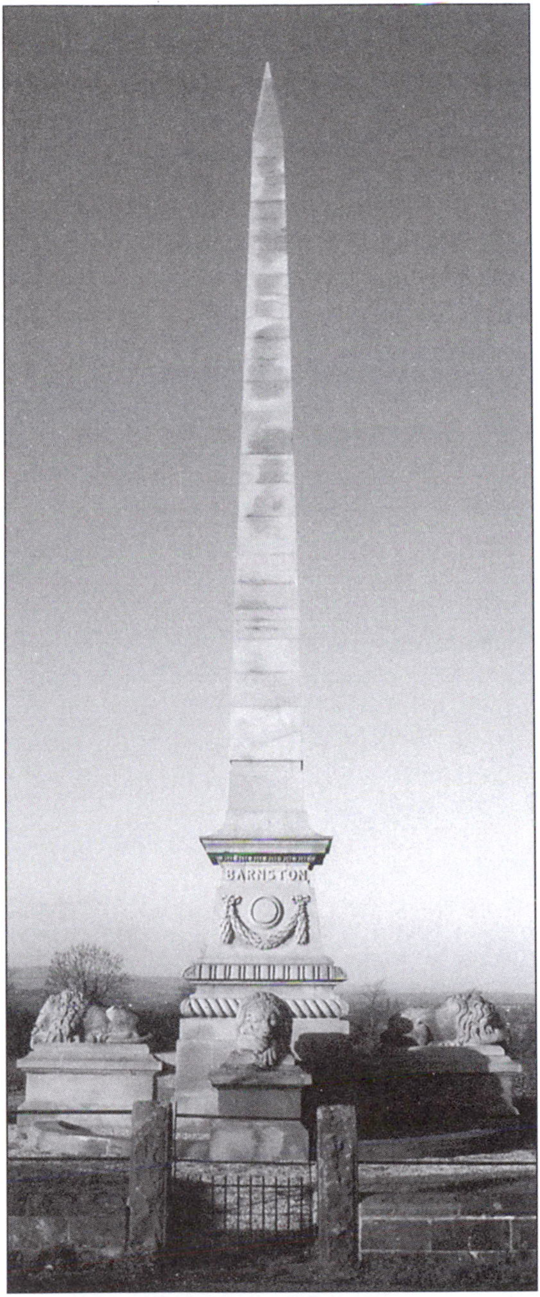

Memories of the Indian Mutiny:
Barnston Memorial

and the church, with its Norman doorway stands on an old crossing route to Wales. A broken cross, probably used for proclamations, hiring labour and completing business agreements, stands in the churchyard with the top step cut in one corner possibly to hold a container of disinfectant to combat plague in a similar manner to others near Macclesfield.

The A41 Chester to Whitchurch road follows an almost straight course as it nears Broxton and the junction with the A 534 Nantwich to Wrexham Road. Proof that the highway has not always followed the present line can be found on the short section of road which "cuts the corner" from the present lay out.

On the apex of a bend stands an imposing stone more like a grave stone rather than its true purpose, that of a mile stone.

Dated 1761 the stone makes its purpose very clearly and brooks no mistake. "This marks the half way house between Chester and Whitchurch, 10 miles each".

Bickerton, beside the

A41 Whitchurch road, is on a wooded ridge overlooking the road from Wales. It is easy to realise the strategic importance of this position and why our ancestors built the Iron Age fort of Maiden Castle here. Any potential enemy approaching from either Wales or from Wirral would be visible in ample time to enable those in the fort to decide between fighting or fleeing.

Still very imposing this defensive position was constructed about the same time as others at Helsby and Eddisbury and like them was brought back into use when the Viking threat was at its height. The position of Maiden Castle also provides a clear line of sight to the other forts.

The hills along the Bickerton ridge provide excellent walking and near the fort can be found a cave known as "Mad Allen's Hole". This was the home of a young man at the start of the 19th century. It is not known exactly who this character was but it is believed that he may have become a hermit as a revolt against parental displeasure of his desired marriage. Alternatively, after the fashion of the day, he may have been paid or encouraged to become a hermit in order to provide interest in an estate in much the same way that follies were constructed to add interest to a particular view.

Between Broxton and Whitchurch and alongside a stretch of the old A41 road lies an ancient pub, the Blue Bell inn. Standing at the quaintly named "Bell o' th' Hill" at Tushingham, it is one of the oldest public houses in the county. The present building dates back to 1667 but was built onto an earlier inn from the 14th century. With no games machines and selling real ale, this establishment has no need for synthetic atmosphere. Whilst many old halls have ghosts and spectres this pub is different. The resident spook is a duck! Whilst alive the bird was adopted as a pet, but it made a nuisance of itself by attacking customers' ankles.

After a brief trial, the web-footed prisoner was executed and buried under the floor. But the duck did not rest easily and returned in spectre form to continue its attacks. The landlord called in twelve priests who prayed over the ghostly duck which shrank smaller and smaller until it could be pushed into a wine bottle and corked tight. The bottle was then sealed into the walls. One of these days a customer will open a bottle of spirits and get more than they bargained!

A few miles from Bickerton, at the tiny village of Peckforton, an attractive country cottage is the host to a beautifully carved stone elephant carrying a castle on its back. An ideal brain teaser, this creation, unfortunately, does not reflect a previously unknown

The Blue Bell Inn, Tushingham

indigenous population of exotic beasts but was created about 1859 by a mason called either William or John Watson who was, apparently, a foreman mason during the construction of the Grosvenor Bridge at Chester. It is believed to have been built as a beehive.

Overlooking the elephant is Peckforton Castle, which is a perfect example of a 13th-century castle. The passage of the centuries has had little effect on the structure of this castle, which is not altogether surprising, as it was only built in 1841 by John Tollemache who, by 1871, was the largest landowner in the county. The castle has featured in a number of films including one featuring that well known hero Robin Hood.

Nearby Beeston Castle is clearly much older and is largely ruined. Constructed by Randle Blundeville, Earl of Chester in about 1220 the castle did not feature in any large battle but was largely destroyed during the civil war.

In the early 16th century the castle was described as being in very poor condition but almost one hundred years later, in 1643, a force of 300 Roundheads occupied the castle. A garrison of eighty secured the site but they were routed by a surprise attack by a force of Royalists. The Roundhead commander was not well received at Nantwich when he rejoined his comrades and was shot as a traitor. The Royalists force had comprised only eight men! The Roundheads later recaptured the castle and ensured that it would be of no further use by destroying the walls.

For those visitors who like adventure, the treasury of Richard II is reputed to be buried within the castle grounds and is still waiting to be found.

Alongside the A49 and a few miles south of Beeston lies a fascinating old cottage with several plaques or images on the walls. The cottage is reputed to have been built on common land using an unofficial rule which allowed such a building to remain if it was constructed between sunset and sunrise and had smoke issuing from the chimney by dawn. Although such a rule was never part of national law it was practised as a local custom in many areas.

A previous owner of the cottage was transported for poaching on the estate of the local landowner. On his return he made the plaques carrying the images of the landowner, gamekeeper magistrate and others involved in his trial together with an image of the devil to put an "evil eye" on them.

Nearby Tarporley has changed tremendously in recent years and has really come to life since the heavy traffic on the A51 has been removed from the main street. The village contains many interesting buildings and features, two of which have particular appeal. "The Swan" is famous for being the meeting place of the Tarporley Hunt, which is the oldest surviving hunting club in England having been founded in 1762.

The Chocolate Shop is situated in the Jubilee Building, built in 1897. It has enjoyed a varied life, housing British and American troops during the war. Between 1957 and 1992, it was the home of the Tarporley Fire Brigade, one of the first volunteer Brigades.

Very popular with tourists who can appreciate the many historic and attractive buildings, Nantwich has many interesting but less obvious links with the past. The scene of an important battle during the civil war, Nantwich was held by the forces of parliament and besieged for two months from November 1643 until January 1644. The failure of the Royalist forces to take Nantwich proved a major victory for Parliament. The main battle took place near the line of the present A500 road between Barony fields and Blue Stone cross-roads.

The town contains a reminder of a more recent conflict. Near the River Weaver and close to Shrewbridge Road lies the grave of Lieutenant Arthur Lesley Brown of the United States Army Air Force who was killed on the 14th January 1944. The airman was flying his P47 Thunderbolt when he encountered sever problems. Witnesses stated that instead of bailing out he chose to remain in his aircraft and steer it away from the town. The grave is situated at the point where the aircraft crashed as neither it, nor the pilot, were recovered due to the quicksand alongside the river. When I first visited there were fresh flowers on the grave but this fact had little significance until a telephone call caused me to look more closely into what happened on that winter day many years ago.

Lesley, as he was known to the family, came from Orangeburg in New York State. He was 23 years old at the time of his death and stationed with the 395 Fighter Training Unit, 6th Fighter Wing, United States Army Air Force based at Atcham near Shrewsbury. The unit was equipped with Republic P47 Thunderbolt fighters which, together with the North American Mustang, provided fighter protection to the long range daylight bombing missions carried out by the American Air Force deep into Germany. This task required the fighters to fly at great heights necessitating the use of oxygen for long periods. The reason for the crash was never discovered but it was thought that one of the objects of the flight was to test the oxygen equipment.

One of the local people who saw the aeroplane moments before it crashed was Mrs Hollowood, now Mrs Gladys Henshall, the Brown Owl of the 4th Nantwich Brownie Pack who met at the Methodist Church in Beam Street, Nantwich. The following weekend the Brownies laid flowers at the scene of the crash.

Ever since the day that Lesley Brown died there have been flowers at the grave. For many years, members of the Brownie Pack laid the flowers and then the practice was continued by Mrs Henshall and by Mrs Margaret Brown who, as an eight-year-old Brownie was a member of the party which laid the first flowers in 1944. At times assistance is given by Mrs Brown's daughter Susan Bebbington and her grandchildren Hannah and Aimee. Flowers are replaced twice a month even though this can be difficult especially in the winter.

Soon after the crash, Mrs Henshall made contact with Lesley's parents Richard and Nettie Brown, resulting in a warm relationship between them and the people of Nantwich which continued for the remainder of their lives. A memorial was created in 1945 with the land being donated by the farmer Mr Philip George who had lost a nephew in the Battle of Britain.

In 1956 Mr and Mrs Brown together with their daughter Dorothy visited the grave and again in 1969 when the people of Nantwich named a new road in honour of their son.

A garden of Remembrance at the site was dedicated in 1985 with representatives from America present and a local stonemason Frank Mason made a new gravestone. The grave and memorial garden have been maintained by the Nantwich and District Branch of the Cheshire Regiment Association since 1965. Each year, on Armistice Day, a special ceremony is carried out at the grave between the ceremonies at Crewe and at Nantwich War memorials.

Further along the river bank is one of the original brine springs which were very important in the growth of the town. Although the Romans found Middlewich and Northwich more important, the salt was certainly exploited by them. The spring is still used to supply water to the nearby swimming baths, which are one of the last remaining open air brine baths in the country.

The beautiful church of St Mary, which was founded soon after the Norman conquest but reconstructed in the 14th and 15th centuries, dominates the centre of the town. During the civil wars the Church was twice used as a prison to hold Royalist troops captured during the battles in the vicinity. Some died in captivity and over 180 bodies from this time are believed to have been buried there.

Captain Thomas Steele, who surrendered Beeston Castle to the Royalist intruders was shot in Tynkers Croft behind the church and then immediately buried in the churchyard.

Visitors to "The Lamb", close to the church, may not realise that they are dining in what was the headquarters of Parliamentary forces during the civil war. The civil war involved most of Britain and lead

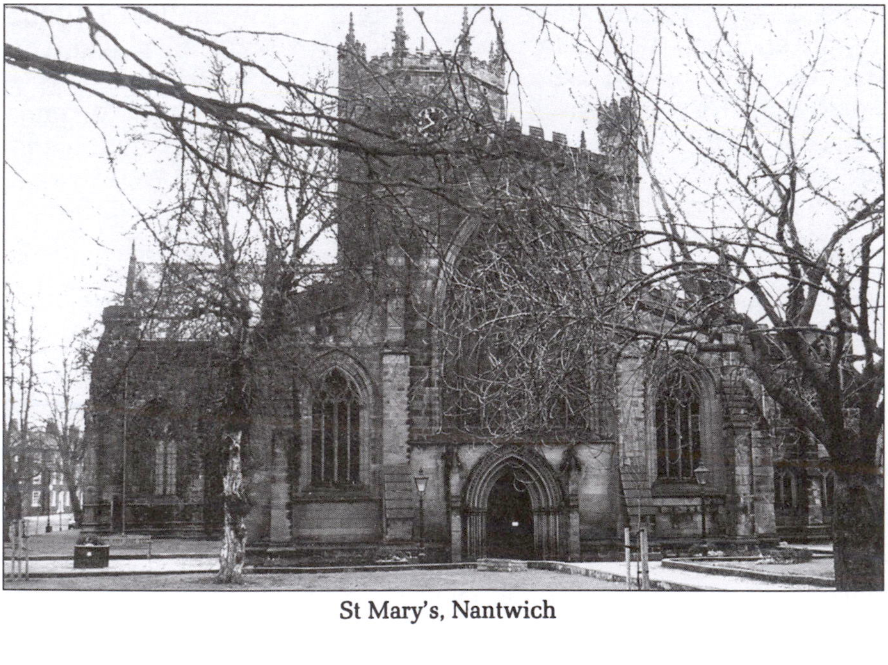

St Mary's, Nantwich

to tremendous hardships. Cheshire was heavily involved, with major battles taking place at Nantwich, Chester and Warrington which were all subjected to long sieges, suffering considerable damage to both life and property. Smaller skirmishes took place in many towns and villages throughout the county.

Chester was the centre for the Royalist forces whilst Nantwich became the headquarters of the forces supporting Parliament. The county was important due to its position. Chester was on the main communication routes from Wales and Ireland, both strongly in support of the King, whilst Nantwich was squarely situated on the land routes between the north and south of England.

The church of St Mary overlooks the traffic-free centre, which includes a shop, ironically selling cigarettes, known as "Queens Aid House". On the first floor a plaque recalls the great fire of 1583 which destroyed 132 properties and killed three women. In the panic it appears that someone released four dancing bears, which were kept nearby as street entertainment. The bears must have added excitement to an already interesting evening.

The importance of Nantwich and the extent of the damaged can be judged by the £1,000 donated by Queen Elizabeth as a personal donation to launch a public appeal to assist the rebuilding of the town. The Queen also provided timber from the Royal Forest at Delamere.

Sweet Briar Hall, which can be found in Hospital Street, was lucky to escape the great fire despite the fact that the building next door was damaged in the inferno. Parts of this fascinating black-and-white building date back to the late 15th century whilst the octagonal bay window was added a century later. Between 1758 and 1761 Sweet Briar Hall is reputed to have been the home of Joseph Priestley, a Unitarian Minister credited with discovering oxygen.

The town square was the site of the gibbet, where those guilty of various crimes were executed. During the civil war a law was enacted making it a capital offence for an Irishman to be carrying arms. Some loyal Irish soldiers were executed by their own comrades.

Although it now appears strange for Nantwich to have housed dancing bears they feature several times in local history. Congleton is still known as "Bear Town" after reputably selling the town Bible to purchase a new animal whilst Audlem near the Shropshire border features a large bear stone next to the church. This stone was used to chain the bears whilst they performed for the local inhabitants. Respectable looking Bunbury near Nantwich still has the remains of a bear pit where fights would be staged between a bear and dogs for the "entertainment" of the local populace.

The Market Hall in Audlem stands in front of the Parish Church, which dates from 1733. The Hall is known as the Butter Hall reflecting the importance of dairy products in the local farming community. Cheshire and, in particular, the area near Audlem, is still one of the leading dairy producers in the country although in recent years the industry has declined considerably. The Foot and Mouth epidemic in 1967 will always be remembered by anyone involved in the operation. Whole herds, many of which had been managed by the same family for centuries, had to be destroyed if one beast became infected. It seemed incredible that one day the fields were full of grazing cattle and the next, they were empty. The sky was full of smoke and the smell of the burning herds lay heavy across the land.

The imposition of milk quotas and then the restrictions resulting from the B.S.E. epidemic has had a major effect on the dairy industry, which is now increasingly dependent on European policy. Many traditional farmers are seeking an alternative direction.

The Shropshire Union canal passes through Audlem and drops 93 feet by means of 15 locks. On a hot summers day the effort of opening the lock gates is exhausting. Although I have never actually opened a lock in my life, the sight of such effort is sufficient to force me to seek refreshment from the local hostelry whilst I recover.

Between Audlem and the county border at Whitchurch are the remains of the Cistercian Abbey of Combermere. Founded in 1173 monks from the Abbey would walk the six miles to Acton near Nantwich for daily devotions. Displaying some of the rather strange habits later found in the Abbots of Vale Royal, the Charter of the Abbey was suspended for a time in 1414 following the discovery that the Abbot had taken to raising funds by making his own. Monarchs tend to take a dim view of counterfeiting. The Abbey was dissolved in 1538. Combermere is the largest privately owned lake in England.

Map References

Barnston Memorial: SJ 413552

Maiden Castle: SJ 495529

Mad Allen's Hole: SJ 507536

Mile Stone: SJ 487551

Blue Bell Public House: SJ 523454

Combermere Abbey: SJ 588442

Elephant and Castle: SJ 538567

Grave of American Airman: SJ 649514

Chapter Seven

Salt and the growth of Religion

Middlewich, Winsford, Vale Royal, Sandbach, Barthomley, Hassall Green, Mow Cop and Congleton

Even before the Romans arrived, Cheshire salt was being traded across many of the tribal boundaries that divided the country. The importance of Middlewich to the Romans is born out by the name they gave to the town, "Salinae", and the fact that production appears to have been much greater than that required in the immediate area. It is believed that salt was part of the "salary" of the Roman soldier ('sal' in both Salinae and salary means salt). Remains of containers of salt from the Middlewich area have been found in the Midlands and near Bristol. Today the piles of salt alongside the Sandbach road testify that the need for salt has not passed even if the methods of extracting the substance have changed. Little remains of the older rock salt industry in Middlewich but the careful observer can find the top of an old shaft head protruding above the roof of a council building.

Nearby Winsford is the home of the only remaining rock salt mine in England, with another at Carrickfergus, Northern Ireland. The Meadow bank mine was home to many of the countries treasures during the war as the dry atmosphere proved ideal protection against damp whilst the good Cheshire earth protected against the attentions of the *Luftwaffe*.

A visit to the mine is an unforgettable experience. It is the sheer size of the workings, which are so awesome. Instead of walking, the visitor is carried along broad tunnels in large road trucks, which are dwarfed by the cutting machines used at the face. The underground roadways are so vast that the light produced by the full headlamps of the vehicles is swallowed, without trace, by the darkness. The working areas bear more resemblance to a cathedral than a working mine.

Vehicles and machines are taken underground in sections before being assembled and at the end of their working lives, instead of being brought to the surface, they are left in old sections of the mine.

Salt town: Middlewich

The salt mined at Meadow bank is used to keep the countries roads free of ice in winter.

Until recently salt was produced at a number of sites throughout Cheshire and the legacy of the work can be seen in the many meres which now add to the scenic views and recreational areas of the county.

The 15th-century parish church of St Chad is situated by the side of the road from Winsford to Church Minshull. The position of the church on the outskirts of Winsford appears somewhat unusual but local history records the fact that the church was originally situated in the centre of the town. One dark night, whilst the good people of Winsford were fast asleep, the church was stolen by the devil who flew off with the building clutched in his arms. The local monks at Vale Royal Abbey, who had witnessed the event, sounded their bells in alarm and alerting St Chad, who intervened. The Devil was so surprised that he dropped the church, which was caught by St Chad and lowered safely to earth to land in its present position. Despite enquiries, the Cheshire Constabulary have yet to make an arrest!

The administrative area in the centre of Cheshire is known as Vale Royal yet many residents are unaware of the reasons which lie behind the choice of name. The village of Whitegate is situated at the entrance to what were the grounds and estate of the greatest Cistercian Monastery in Britain. Apart from a few stones and the name, little remains of the Abbey which was over 40 feet longer than Fountains Abbey. The present hall, which is now a hotel and golf club, was built much later.

King Edward 1st, whilst still the Prince of Wales was returning from the Crusades when his ship was struck by a tremendous storm. In imminent fear of death, Edward promised that if he survived he would build a centre for worship in Cheshire. Edward was the Royal Earl of the county.

In 1264 Edward together with his father King Henry III were held prisoner by Simon de Montford and were well looked after by monks of the Cistercian order. This experience reminded Edward of his promise and the first stone of the new Abbey was laid in 1277 being consecrated by the Bishop of St Asaph in the presence of King Edward and Queen Eleanor. A nucleus of 100 monks started at Dernhall, now Darnhall, with the move into the new location taking place in 1330. The Royal Charter giving protection to the Order was granted in 1299.

It is easy today to think of an Abbey as a quiet centre of religious contemplation with groups of monks carrying out good work in the local community. In the case of Vale Royal the reality appears to have been very different with the monks being hated and feared by the majority of the population.

The Royal Charter gave the Abbot the power to raise money from the local population, the rights of life and death within the boundaries of the estate and virtual immunity from the laws of the land.

Taxation was imposed, products sold outside the estate required permission as did the marriage of a daughter. The local population, who had enough problems trying to earn a living, found themselves having to fund a large and expensive Abbey which it is very clear, abused the power given by the King. The Abbey took over 50 years to complete and cost more than £50,000 at that time. It is difficult to imagine a comparative cost today.

The people of Cheshire were not renown as being easy subjects and they certainly resented the extravagance of the monks. Before the Abbey was dissolved in 1536 there were fourteen Abbots. Local people tried to curtail the power of the Abbots by taking them before the courts but failed as the Charter granted the monks almost total power. Frustrated and desperate several Abbots had attempts made on their lives. One Abbot was charged with harbouring bands of robbers and another charged with stealing the property of the Abbey. One monk was murdered with his head being used in a game of football.

The subservient Knights of the estate also protested against the excesses of the Abbots but to little avail as once again the Charter protected the monks.

When Henry VIII dissolved the monasteries it certainly met with the approval of many in Cheshire. Hefferston Grange at Weaverham and Knights Grange are reminders of a time when the powers of the church were abused.

A grave in the churchyard at Elworth near Sandbach illustrates the dangers often faced by the Police. Constable James Green was murdered on duty on 24th February 1873 whilst investigating a case of poaching. The tragedy of the event was made worse by the death of his young wife only a few months later in June. Despite a subsequent court case nobody was ever convicted of the crime. Constable Green is the only Officer of the Cheshire Constabulary who is recorded as having been murdered on duty (one other officer is believed to have been murdered but the inquest verdict was not conclusive).

Sandbach is a market town lying in the south of the county with an excellent Thursday market attracting people from many parts of Cheshire and neighbouring Staffordshire. The market itself stands on the old common near the town centre which is known locally as "Scotch Common". A visitor can wander the numerous stalls displaying a wide selection of goods.

In 1651 Scottish soldiers returning from the defeat at the battle of Worcester camped overnight on the common. Reported to have been in a poor state, hungry, exhausted and with some injured men amongst them, they were attacked by local people in the dark and "the cobbles ran red with Scottish blood".

In the centre of the town is the cobbled square on which stand two Saxon crosses, the larger of the two is over 16 feet tall whilst the smaller is 10 feet 6 inches high. It is believed that originally there were three crosses dating from the 8th or 9th centuries. The size and nature of the crosses indicate that Sandbach was an important place of worship long before the Norman invasion.

The crosses were destroyed in about 1613 by a group of Puritans and the stones scattered as far as Tarporley and Oulton Park before being recovered in 1816. Several pieces of the old crosses can be found near the doorway to St Mary's Church. Across the road from the church is the Old Hall a half-timbered house dating back to 1656.

Saxon crosses and hog roast, Sandbach

The Hall is now used as a restaurant and legend tells of secret tunnels between the Hall and the Church.

At Hassall Green, near Sandbach, a "Tin Tabernacle" church in a splendid pink colour lies between the canal and the busy M6 motorway. This Church, unlike Winsford, was never stolen but is believed by many to have been moved to its present location in about 1898 after serving the residents of Alsager for several years.

For centuries Alsager was part of the parish of Barthomley but was some miles distant. Christchurch had met the spiritual needs of Alsager but a disagreement arose between the Vicar at Barthomley and the Curate at Christchurch. This had simmered for many years with the vicar of Barthomley providing services on the west of Alsager using a "Tin Tabernacle", or prefabricated building, to provide temporary facilities. In 1882 the Bishop of Chester ruled that the dispute would end and ordered a new parish church to be built at Alsager. The Church of St Mary was built in 1894 and consecrated in 1898.

Many people in Alsager believe that the tin tabernacle then became available and was moved to Hassall Green, where it remains. Unfortunately, illustrations of the old building at Alsager, make it clear that the two buildings are very different. It is not known what became of the former Alsager Church but it was still in position at Alsager when the Hassall Green chapel was in service.

Although only a small but very attractive village, Barthomley, which lies some 3 miles from Alsager, has two claims to fame. The church is a 14th-century building and was the scene of a massacre in 1643 during the civil war. Possibly as a result of a shot being fired at a group of soldiers moving towards Nantwich, Royalist forces entered the village and tried to capture some twenty men who sought refuge in the church. When promised protection the men surrendered but twelve were murdered and the remainder badly wounded. The incident formed one of the charges brought against Charles I during his trial.

Barthomley is also reputed to be the place where the last wolf in England was killed. As with the stories of the Cheshire Cat and the legend of King Canute there are many other claimants, some with a far greater claim to reality. True or false? Who knows?

Many travellers on the M6 motorway in south Cheshire will be familiar with what appears to be a ruined castle standing on an prominent hill. Visible for many miles, the hill is called Mow Cop and the "ruined castle" is known as Wilbraham's Folly. Overlooking both Hassall Green and Sandbach from the high ground marking the

Wilbraham's Folly, Mow Cop

border between Cheshire and Staffordshire, the folly was built by Randle Wilbraham of Rode Hall in 1754. The structure was constructed as it now stands and was never intended to serve a practical purpose having been built both to improve the view and to act as an early employment scheme to assist the local unemployed.

Mow Cop lies on the boundary between Cheshire and Staffordshire, the diocese of Chester and Lichfield and marks the boundary between the archiepiscopal provinces of Canterbury and York.

The importance of Mow Cop is not restricted to acting as a boundary marker for the administration of the Church of England. A large stone beside the car park records that the Primitive Methodist Church was born there on 31st May 1807. Known initially as "The Ranters" the church remained independent until 1932 when it united with the Methodist Church. John Wesley also preached here. It is a shame that modern graffiti has made the commemorative stone difficult to read.

Near Congleton and on the same county boundary lie the Bridestones, a group of massive stones set in a small enclosure a few hundred yards from the road between Congleton and Rushton Spencer. These stones are part of a Neolithic tomb about 4500 years old and were originally covered by earth. The design of the tomb is very similar to others in Wales, Scotland, Ireland and the Isle of Man. Little is known about the people of this age but they are believed to have originated from the Middle East, with their use of stone reflecting some of the Egyptian tombs from that period. As many of the chambers are situated near to the coasts it would appear that these people used the sea for travel and trade but were not restricted to the coast.

On some of the tombs from this period can be found a spiral design. Hand printed onto the stones these markings have lasted for thousands of years. Examples can be found on the stones at Calderstones Park in Liverpool and at Barclodiad y Gawres near Llanfaelog on the Isle of Anglesey. Similar designs can be found in the Temples of Malta which pre-date the Pyramids.

One of the puzzles arising from the Bridestones and the many Neolithic remains found along the Pennine hills is the scarcity of evidence in Cheshire itself. With its proximity to the coast it could be expected that many remains would be found within the county. Some experts believe that the county was sparsely populated due to the many dangerous animals in the woodlands. Sandstone, which is to be found across most of the Cheshire plain, is much softer than the harder rocks of the uplands and it may be that tombs have failed to survive the ravages of time. The Bronze Age, which followed, left many burial mounds and barrows scattered across the county. Perhaps more likely is that as the population on the fertile lowlands grew and farming increased, then stones from the tombs would be used for houses or shelter.

Below the Bridestones lies the town of Congleton, still remembered for selling the town bible in order to purchase a dancing bear for the entertainment of the locals.

Bradshaw House is a distinguished looking house situated on the main street near the town hall. The house stands on the site of the home of a former mayor of the town who gained considerable fame, or notoriety.

John Bradshaw, was born in 1602 in Marple. Educated at Bunbury and at Kings School, Macclesfield he became the mayor of Congleton in 1637, the MP for Cheshire in 1654 and the Chancellor of the Duchy of Lancaster from 1650 – 1655. A very intelligent man he was a firm supporter of Cromwell and was appointed as Lord President of the court which tried King Charles 1st. In his capacity as President, his was the first signature on the Death Warrant. Bradshaw later fell out of favour with Cromwell but remained in a position of considerable power.

After his death in 1659 he was buried in Westminster Hall with full honours. In common with Cromwell he suffered the changes of fate and after death both were dug up, hung on the scaffold, beheaded and whilst their bodies were buried under the scaffold their heads were displayed on spikes at Westminster. There is a church record of his birth which, in addition to recording details of parents, has the single word "Traitor" written alongside.

The British have a strange way of showing their appreciation of former heroes.

On the outskirts of the town near the junction of Newcastle Road and the quaintly named Fol Hollow lies a plague stone.

The word "Plague" is usually associated with Bubonic Plague, which became known as the Black Death after the black or blue coloured swellings or boils in the lymphatic glands that were the visible symptoms of the disease. The Black Death is believed to have killed between a third and half the population of Europe during an outbreak around the year 1349 and records show that many farms in Cheshire were unoccupied after this time. There were periodic outbreaks during the following centuries with a serious outbreak during the

17th century. The Black Death left its legacy in the graves and in the nursery rhyme "Ring a ring of roses". The roses described the symptoms whilst the "pocket full of posies" referred to the herbs and lucky charms brought into service as protection.

In reality the Black Death was only one of many diseases which ravaged the population. Cholera, Typhus, Smallpox and Measles, combined with low standards of hygiene to ensure that many people did not reach old age. Today we bask in the knowledge that we are safe and such times are in the far distant past. A journey to North Wales, however, should dispel any such comfortable belief and act as a reminder that we are not as secure as we might believe.

The "Marble Church" at Bodelwyddan is host to 83 graves of Canadian servicemen. The dates on the stones show that most of them died in 1918 or 1919, at the end or just after the end, of the First World War. The age of the men, who it can be assumed, were in an above-average physical condition, show that youth and fitness were little defence against an outbreak of influenza which struck at the end of the war. The outbreak killed an estimated 20 million people, more than four years of fighting.

Aids and other modern epidemics have already shown that they are capable of mutating to a point where modern medicine has limited effect. These diseases have yet to realise their full potential although they are causing devastating misery in parts of Africa. Complacency is very dangerous and a little thought clearly shows that plagues have not gone away, they will certainly return.

Citizens in the past did not have access to modern medicine and so had to make do with what was available to prevent the spread of the disease. Plague stones were set up on the town boundaries, food would be left at the base of the stone and vinegar or urine poured into the hollow at the top to wash and disinfect coins.

Within a few hundred yards of the plague stone lies the parish church of Astbury. Standing in the centre of the village the church forms a marvellous backdrop to a stunning display of daffodils, which transform the village green every spring. Within the church yard is an ancient Yew tree reputed to be 1000 years old. Many old churches have, or had, Yew trees growing in their grounds but few people know the reason. A regular army is a relatively new concept. When the King required troops he would call on the Lords and their Knights to supply a certain number of armed and trained men and each Parish had to provide those men.

The archers of Cheshire were recognised for their expertise and it was vital that they had sufficient weapons. King Edward 1st passed a law requiring each parish to grow Yew trees in order to ensure the supply of bows. As the sap from the Yew is poisonous to cattle the safest place for the tree was within the walls of the church yard.

One of the most well known buildings in Cheshire lies within the parish of Astbury. Only a few miles inside the county boundary and lying alongside the A34 road, Little Moreton Hall features on numerous calendars, chocolate boxes and books about Cheshire. Built between 1540 and 1559 the house is surrounded by a moat and managed by the National Trust. A visit to the house provides a fascinating experience for the visitor with few walls, if any, standing straight.

The leaning house, Little Moreton Hall

Map References

Mow Cop: SJ 857577

Bridestones: SJ 905622

Plague Stone: SJ 845621

Chapter Eight

Eastern Cheshire and Tablets of Stone

Marton, Gawsworth, Macclesfield, The Macclesfield Canal, Bollington, Disley and Prestbury

Standing by the side of the A34 road a few miles north of Congleton is the parish church of Marton. The 14th-century black-and-white building is an outstanding half-timbered church. Containing mediaeval frescoes, the church is one of the oldest timber framed building in Europe still used for worship. The roof of the church is of Kerridge slab whilst the tower is faced with wooden shingles.

The neighbouring parish of Siddington is also served by a church which, from a distance, is similar in appearance. On closer inspection it can be seen that parts of the outside are of painted brick. Built slightly later than Marton, the church was also half-timbered but much of the original structure has been protected by a brick casing to prevent further deterioration. Both Marton and Siddington are beautifully maintained and present an attractive picture to all who pass along the busy A34.

Marton church and broken cross

Between Siddington and the nearby town of Macclesfield lies Gawsworth with two halls, four fish pools and one lovely old church. The old hall is the most widely known and hosts musical and theatrical events in its grounds during the summer months. Both the hall and the church can be viewed across the fish pools where fish were farmed to provide food for the tables of the hall. On a summers evening the lawns of the hall stretch down to the waters edge and are host to numerous visitors who can enjoy a full picnic before listening to music in the most idyllic setting.

The hall was the home of the Fitton family who served the crown with distinction over many centuries taking part in most of the wars including a considerable involvement in Ireland. Sir Edward Fitton, who died in 1572, is buried in Dublin. His son, also named Edward, was the president of Munster. Edward's daughter Mary was maid of honour to Queen Mary and was reputed to be the dark lady of Shakespeare's sonnets. The Queen's court was famous for being one of the most disreputable in Europe yet Mary Fitton was apparently expelled for unacceptable behaviour. She must have been quite a character.

The hall has a mediaeval jousting ground and in the nearby wood is the grave of Maggoty Johnson. Born in 1691 Johnson was a dance teacher who achieved success by writing a play in which he played the leading role as Lord Flame. The play was a great success in 1729 but appears to have turned his head. Arriving in Gawsworth in 1740 he seems to have been regarded as an eccentric character requiring the locals to address him as "My Lord Flame".

Before he died in 1773 he wrote his own epitaph and was buried in the nearby woods. It appeared that the local gentry did not take to kindly to the epitaph written by Johnson so Lady Harrington decided to have the last word and in 1851 wrote a more suitable epitaph which is inscribed on a stone alongside the original. Whether or not Lady Harrington will have the last word has yet to be decided as there have been reports that Maggoty Johnson's ghost has been seen in nearby lanes!

Gawsworth New Hall, built in the 18th century, is a proud building in its own right. One of its more famous and flamboyant residents was Lord Mohun who was twice charged with murder and then, in 1712, fought a duel with the Duke of Hamilton in Hyde Park. Both men were killed.

Overlooking both Gawsworth and Macclesfield are the peaks of the Pennines. Shinning Tor, the highest point in Cheshire, and the Cat and Fiddle, the second highest public house in England, mark the boundary with Derbyshire.

Along the Eastern boundary of the county the whole nature of Cheshire changes with the undulating fields replaced by the Pennine Hills The soft colour of sandstone is replaced by the harder grey and hawthorn hedges are replaced by stone walls. Agriculture reflects the harsher conditions to be found here in winter and, perhaps because of this, many features have remained unchanged for years longer than on the more intensively farmed fields of the Cheshire plain.

Macclesfield, also known as "Treacle Town", after a road accident involving barrels of molasses, is famous as a centre for the silk industry but has several other less obvious claims to fame. Cumberland House in Jordansgate, now a Doctor's surgery, provided accommodation for the Duke of Cumberland who stayed there in 1745 during his pursuit of Bonnie Prince Charlie who was retreating to Scotland after the defeat at Worcester.

It is reported that in 1799 Macclesfield was the last place in England to hold a wives' auction. Two ladies went for half a crown and one shilling respectively. Although never legal, this practice was reported to be quite widespread. I thought the idea might be worth reviving. I am not sure if my wife agrees or not as she is no longer speaking to me!

The town has several public parks, but West Park has a bowling green which is unusual both in shape and size and is reputed to be the largest in England.

For those who enjoy a good walk in the countryside with plenty of wildlife and excellent views, the Macclesfield canal is a must. The canal follows a winding course half way up a ridge, passing through woods and fields. Difficult to locate but still visible are traces of the mines and industry, which were the reasons for the construction of the canal.

Near the point where the canal is crossed by the Macclesfield to Buxton road, stands a large mill. Originally built in 1820 as a steam operated corn mill, the building provides accommodation for several local firms. Its position alongside the canal meant that it could be serviced by the many working boats on the canal. Today one or two work boats can still be found but the neighbouring marina is full of boats used for holidays rather than commerce. Although there is nothing to distinguish this mill from others of the same period it was here in 1885 that the world's first Hovis loaf was created.

The Macclesfield Canal was one of the last of the narrow canals to be constructed. The 28-mile canal, designed to improve communication between Manchester and the Potteries, opened in 1831 joining Marple and Kidsgrove. Planned by Thomas Telford, the canal was built by William Crosley and carried coal from the mines at Poynton and Adlington to Macclesfield until the railway arrived in 1845. The

The Hovis Mill, Macclesfield

Anson and Park Pits, which were near Poynton, operated twenty boats carrying coal in 1847.

Near to the town and lying next to the canal is Gurnett. Alongside the road a house bears a plaque recording that James Brindley, who lived from 1716 to 1772, stayed here whilst he carried out his apprenticeship to Abraham Bennett. Brindley was one of the leading engineers of the canal era. Some stories relate that Brindley had great difficulty reading and writing but overcame that handicap by retaining and calculating many problems in his head.

It is a commonly held belief that in the summers of old, the sun was always shinning and life resembled a painting by Constable. A short journey along the county boundary from Disley to Macclesfield and Congleton looking at evidence recorded on stones can produce sufficient evidence to make us reconsider some of our preconceived ideas.

Standing in the centre of the children's play area in West Park, are three crosses, brought to the town from Macclesfield Forest. They are thought to have been erected before the Norman invasion when Cheshire was part of Mercia. Standing some six feet high and missing their heads, these crosses are impressive but it is clear that they do not belong in their present position where they lack dignity and are

Mercian crosses in West Park, Macclesfield

very liable to be damaged. Similar crosses exist at Leek in Staffordshire, at Cleulow Cross on the road between Congleton and Buxton and at Llangollen in North Wales.

Fragments of Mercian crosses can be found at several locations throughout the county and it may be that their size and nature made them particularly liable to attack by puritan zealots in the 17th century.

It is not certain what purpose the crosses originally served but it is thought that some were placed near the main trade routes to act as markers and to encourage piety amongst the traders and other travellers. Market crosses were intended to act as a focal point for the community and it was from them that proclamations would be made and business deals agreed. They sometimes acted as the meeting point for the hiring of labour, the cross at Greasby in Wirral is an example. This role in trade would also explain why some crosses would be used as plague stones.

When travelling from Bosley towards Buxton the road climbs as it reaches the lower slopes of the Pennines. The rolling fields start to be replaced with heather and the horizon widens revealing stunning views. At Cleulow Cross a knoll appears with trees crowding around the top. Even on a sunny day the top of the knoll is in shadow with brief breaks in the canopy allowing sunlight to shine through and play on the large Mercian cross in the centre. As with those at Macclesfield this cross has also lost its head.

It is clear that this is the proper location for such a monument. The atmosphere is electric and stirs the imagination.

The passage of the years has mellowed the stone but traces of its original ornate carvings can be found near the top. I must admit that I have considerable reservations concerning the antiquity of the swastika carved mid way up the column. In one corner of the base stone there appears to be a bowl-like depression which may indicate that the cross was used as a plague stone.

Similar depressions in the base stones of crosses can be found on the Bow Stones near Disley and at Shocklach on the Welsh border, whilst plague stones can be found at Congleton, Warrington and next to the old saltersway between Whaley Bridge and Bow Stones. The later, which is near the Moorside Hotel, is shown on maps as "The Dipping Stone" which is a clear indication of its purpose.

Between Sutton and Wildboarclough lies the Greenway Cross, which is thought to be older than the Cleulow Cross, possibly from the 9th or 10th century. The design shows the influence of Norse culture although some experts believe they may have been of pagan

The Dipping Stone, near Disley

origin before being converted to Christianity. This cross stands near the junction of two ancient roads and is also believed to have been used as a plague stone. The "disinfectant" would have been placed in a bowl next to the cross.

The Bow Stones lie on the ridge overlooking Lyme Park and are by the side of the same old highway to Whaley Bridge as the Dipping Stone. The stones were "discovered" in Disley Church in 1956 and replaced in their present positions where it is believed they have stood since the 16th century. Very different in appearance from both the Greenway and Cleulow crosses, these form a pair.

It is possible that the Bow Stones may have been the top sections of Mercian crosses later used as Preaching Crosses, from where travelling preachers would address the residents of rural communities.

All the crosses standing in their original locations are near old trading routes. Usually at the top of steep inclines and enjoying tremendous views they have a sense of purpose and belonging. They must have given the traders of old a welcome opportunity to rest and perhaps consider the more spiritual aspects of life whilst recovering their breath.

The plague stones themselves are far more functional in appearance having been made purely for the purpose of disease control. At first sight both the Congleton and Warrington stones resemble bird baths whilst the Dipping Stone has two hollows in the centre of a large square stone.

The reason for the plague stones is shown by two groups of graves lying in fields near to the ridge at Bow Stones. Although the writing is now very faint and in places impossible to read, one group of stones recalls the Hampson family of two adults and three children who lie together in the corner of a field, having died in 1646. The second stone in this group seems to speak to the reader as it states:

"Think not strange our bones lye here. Thine may lye thou knowest not where. Elizabeth Hampson."

Some distance away, three similar gravestones record the resting-place of others who died in the same period.

None of the graves is in consecrated ground and it is thought they were of families who lived in nearby cottages close to the old highway and probably caught the plague from travellers on the road. The very real fear of infection meant that plague victims were often buried in considerable haste and often with little ceremony.

People were not only at risk from disease. In Prestbury lies the body of William Wyatt who was "shot through" whilst attempting to arrest two highway robbers at Shrigley in 1848. William's brother Thomas was badly injured in the same incident.

The subject of the attack was a Mr Ernill from Macclesfield who had left Poynton to collect debts from customers. Mr Ernill resisted when attacked and the Wyatt brothers went to assist. The murderer was later hanged.

The churchyard is also recorded as being the final resting place of an Edward Green who was murdered in 1750 by a highwayman. Despite a diligent search I have not been able to locate the grave.

At Rainow and at Higher Disley there are murder stones set by the roadside, which record murders that occurred at that location. At Rainow the stone records the death of John Turner in 1735 (the present stone shows 1755), whilst at Disley the stone, which lies by the side of the Disley to Whaley Bridge road recalls the murder of William Wood of Evam (Ilam) in Derbyshire on July 16th 1823. Passers by are cheerfully warned "Prepare to meet thy God".

Murder stone near Disley

The Highwayman Public House, on the Macclesfield to Whaley Bridge road, is reputed to have been named after a local villain who would wait at Pym Chair, which lies on the top of the ridge overlooking the road. He could observe "trade" approaching from either direction before riding down to the crossroads near the Public House where he would strike.

The very common use of the death penalty for many offences which today we would consider trivial, did little to prevent crime. The cinema has done much to turn the Highwayman into a dashing, romantic figure. In reality the roads were not safe for honest travellers and the risk of becoming the victim of very serious crime must have made life difficult for those whose livelihoods depended on travelling the roads. Many people believe strongly that Highway robbery has not so much disappeared as been taken over by the Government in the form of taxation.

The risk of highway robbery, disease and the quaint old habit of hanging people and then leaving the bodies for months, hanging on the gibbet set by the roadside must have made a walk in the countryside an interesting experience. The present century does have its drawbacks, but ... !

Stones were also used simply to mark the boundary of a township and an example, resembling a mile stone, can be found on the old Macclesfield to Buxton road near to the entrance to Teggs Nose Country Park. A less formal example is the Merestone found near the Saddlebore mine at Alderley Edge.

Remembering Waterloo: White Nancy

To the north of Macclesfield lies "Happy Valley", or, as it is more correctly known, Bollington. The town lies in a steep valley and retains some of its mills, a legacy of its industrial past. Overlooking the houses and set high on a hill is a conical shaped structure known as "White Nancy". The "White" refers to its usual colour although at times of national importance, such as the Football World Cup, it has been known to change to suitable colours whilst at Christmas a splendid Christmas Pudding can sometimes be seen.

Built to commemorate the Battle of Waterloo in 1815, the structure was completed in 1817 by John Gaskell of North End Farm. Fitted with an access door and furniture it enabled the family to enjoy a picnic whilst taking in the view across Bollington and the Cheshire Plain. It was only in recent times that vandalism made it essential to seal the doorway.

Standing in the dark by White Nancy the observer may see a flickering light in nearby Pott Shrigley. On the corner in the centre of the village is a solitary gas lamp, which still uses gas and not electricity.

Local residents assure me that this is the last working gas lamp in the country. The supply is provided by the neighbouring house owner.

A public footpath from Bollington to Marple follows the line of the old Macclesfield, Bollington and Marple Railway which opened in 1869. The Middlewood Way, like the Wirral Way, is a fine example of using redundant railway lines for such purposes. A walk along the path to Poynton with the return along the Macclesfield canal is not only very enjoyable but also passes the sites of the old coal mines at Poynton and Adlington. Although a vision of walking through old mine buildings may be alarming, there is in fact, only a few traces of the old pits and then only apparent to the keen searcher.

The Parish Church of Pott Shrigley housed a lending library at the end of the 15th century. Above both Pott Shrigley and Bollington the countryside becomes wilder and in winter can be both extremely beautiful and dangerous. Near Lamaload reservoir a murder stone, referred to earlier, recalls a local mystery.

On Christmas Eve 1735, 29-year-old John Turner, of nearby Saltersford Hall, was returning home with his mule team for Christmas. Despite a severe snow storm he refused to shelter in Bollington and carried on his journey. His body was found the next day and the stone records that next to his body was found the imprint of a woman's shoe. The stone is apparently the third and records the date incorrectly as 1755. There does not appear to be any record of how Turner was killed, the identity of the woman, or, why there was the imprint of only one shoe! Maybe she only had one leg!

Map References

Cleulow Cross: SJ 952674

Greenway Cross: SJ 956693

Dipping Stone: SJ 995817

Bow Stones: SJ 973813

White Nancy: SJ 939772

Murder Stone, Rainow: SJ 978759

Murder Stone, Disley: SJ 995827

Chapter Nine

From The Bronze Age to The Space Age

Jodrell Bank, Wilmslow, Alderley Edge, Chelford, Mobberley, Holmes Chapel, Byley, Cranage and Toft

Looming high over the Cheshire countryside between Holmes Chapel and Chelford is the immense structure of Jodrell Bank Radio Telescope. The 250 foot bowl is supported by metal towers 180 feet high and is operated by Manchester University. In theory this huge structure, which was built in 1957, should appear totally out of place in this most rural of areas but in fact the telescope seems to belong amongst the fields and country lanes. For many years the telescope has been at the centre of research into distant space and played an important role in tracking early Russian space vehicles. Few people

Jodrell Bank Radio Telescope

realise that part of the telescope has a much earlier connection with Russia and with events that shaped the modern world.

The massive size of the telescope meant that the engineering problems involved in the construction were considerable. The huge bowl of the receiver has to be able to be aligned in the vertical as well as the horizontal plane, to enable distant signals to be received with maximum efficiency. The strength required at the points where the bowl pivots on the upright towers of the structure is immense.

When the telescope was being constructed, suitable rack and pinion fittings were located by courtesy of the Royal Navy. Two battleships *HMS Royal Sovereign* and *HMS Revenge* were being scrapped and the mounting rings, which enabled the gun turrets to rotate and follow a target, were available. Capable of withstanding the massive forces generated when three fifteen-inch guns fired simultaneously, they were ideal for their new role.

HMS Royal Sovereign had been built in 1916, was present at the surrender of the German High Seas Fleet in 1918 and served as escort for many convoys during the Second World War before being lent to Russia where she served in the Russian Navy from 1944 until 1949.

By the side of the public library in Wilmslow is an old green and white horse-drawn caravan. This is the memorial to Rev George Bramwell Evens or "Romany", who was a regular radio broadcaster on Children's Hour during the 1920s and 1930s. Of Romany extraction, he introduced children to the countryside and encouraged them to take an interest in rural matters. Surrounded by a small but well maintained park, the location is a fine memorial to a gentleman who loved the countryside and helped others to share that love.

"Romany" would have loved Lindow Common which lies only a mile from his caravan and which he would have known during his lifetime. An ancient bog, it was the grave of "Wilmslow Pete" or "Lindow Man" who was murdered and buried in the bog two thousand years ago.

The true story of Lindow Man involves three deaths separated by two millennia. In 1983, information was received by the Cheshire Constabulary that a local man, serving a period of imprisonment, had told a fellow prisoner that he had killed his wife some 15 years earlier. Enquiries confirmed that the lady in question had not been seen for many years and an Officer was dispatched to interview the man concerned. Co-operation was not forthcoming and enquiries continued.

At the time the lady was last seen, the couple lived in a house next to the bog, which is now only a shadow of what must have been a very extensive area. In 1983 the marsh was the site of peat extraction in much the same way as had taken place for hundreds of years.

In May 1983 two men were working preparing the peat for transport when they found an old football or dinosaurs egg. As they joked, some of the peat fell away, revealing eye sockets. A rapid call to the Police Station resulted in a preliminary opinion by a pathologist that the skull was female and about twenty years old.

Two actions then took place very quickly. The same officer was dispatched to the prison to announce the finding of the murder victim and search teams, including my good self, started to search the bog for further parts of the body. Faced with the finding of what everyone believed to be the body of his wife, the prisoner confessed to the killing and was later convicted of manslaughter.

At Lindow bog the search teams sieved tons of peat in the search for bones but none were found. A few days later a more precise test on the skull confirmed that it was in fact female but that death had occurred about AD150. The body of the murdered wife has never been found nor was the body of Lindow woman.

In August 1984 again whilst sieving peat, workmen found part of a human leg. Initially thought to be part of the modern murder, tests and the discovery of a considerable part of the remainder of the body brought the realisation that a very important archaeological discovery had been made.

The latest body was male and had been the subject of a ritual murder approximately 300BC. Immersion in peat bogs was of some religious significance and the body carried the evidence of three methods of execution. A stab wound to the chest, garrotte around the neck and a cut throat certainly ensured that the victim was dead. It is believed that three methods were used to satisfy a trilogy of Gods.

The centre of Mobberley village is small but the parish covers an extensive rural area. The Parish Church of St Wilfrid carries a stained glass window dedicated to an extraordinary member of a very distinguished family. George Herbert Leigh-Mallory was the son of the rector Canon Herbert Leigh-Mallory who was rector from 1885 until 1904. George died aged 38 years in June 1924 whilst attempting a final assault on Mount Everest with his younger companion Andrew Irvine. The body of George Mallory was found on Everest in 1999 but no one can prove whether the two reached the summit before being overwhelmed.

George was not the only member of this remarkable family to achieve eminence. During the Second World War his brother, Air

Mobberley parish church

Vice Marshall Trafford Leigh-Mallory, was the commander of 12 Group during the Battle of Britain and then, on promotion to Air Marshall, led Fighter Command from November 1942. He was killed in a flying accident in November 1944 whilst on the way to take up his new role as Air Commander South East Asia Command.

On the edge of the parish, deep in the fields and away from all modern roads, lies an old Quaker graveyard dating back to the 17th century. Before the Toleration Act of 1689 many religious sects were persecuted for their beliefs which dared to differ from that of the state. About 1654 there lived in the Mobberley area a large Quaker community who were frequently taken before the Church courts and fined or imprisoned in Middlewich goal. The community bought the field for use as a graveyard in 1669 and then extended the site in 1673. The earliest stone readable is in fact dated 1659 and records apparently show that over 400 people were buried in the graveyard.

On the other side of one of the boundary walls lies Graveyard Farm which is now providing facilities for natural burials enabling those who wish, to be buried in less formal surroundings than a churchyard or council cemetery. They may choose instead to lie in a beautiful rural setting with only a tree, shrub or wild flowers to mark their resting place. The access road to both the Quaker graveyard and the farm is an old Drovers Trail used, until the 20th century to drive cattle to the markets at Manchester.

The village of Alderley Edge takes its name from the prominent wooded hill, which overlooks the village and the surrounding countryside. Well known to local residents and to the many visitors who travel from the surrounding counties, the National Trust property at Alderley Edge does not cover a vast area but in terms of interest must rate extremely highly.

There are two sides to the Edge, what you can see and what you cannot. On the surface it is an area of outstanding beauty with an abundance of walks along leafy paths with a plentiful supply of wild life to enliven the proceedings. The paths wind past old abandoned quarry workings, where copper ore was extracted and now young children can run through the leaves and explore the remains in safety.

Information and guidance explaining the story of the Edge, its history, wildlife and features can all be obtained from the National Trust centre near The Wizard Restaurant.

The Edge is a special place because of the many myths and fables that surround this area. One of the most well known concerns King Arthur and the Knights of the Round Table who rest, sleeping deeply, in a huge cave beneath the hill whilst they await the call that England's hour of need is at hand. Upon hearing the call, the Knights will awake, mount the white horses that share their sleep and then, when ready, the rock will split asunder and the Knights will ride forth to save England. There are many mornings when, listening to the news, I can imagine Arthur and his men might start to waken!

The visitor is unlikely to come across King Arthur, unless the it happens to be "That" day although they may well come across horse riders enjoying the colours and peace of the woods. By exploring, the visitor is able to find a magic circle of large stones, a stone of power, known as the Golden Stone and several natural wells producing streams of fresh water. One is situated beneath a carving in the rock of a wizards face and the inscription that the visitor is welcome to "Drink of this and take thy fill, for the water falls by the Wizards will". The carving is clearly the work of Merlin the Wizard who is the guardian of the sleeping knights.

At Stormy Point the trees give way enabling the visitor to gaze across the fields to Manchester and the distant Pennine Hills. Nearby a stone marks the site of a beacon erected as part of a chain covering the whole country to provide warning of invasion by the Spanish

Armada. At Castle Rock the remains of what appears to have been the stone foundations of a fortification of some description have been found although it does not appear that construction was continued after the first stage. It has been suggested that the site was an alternative to Beeston Castle and was intended to protect against the Welsh. Whilst it is most certainly in the wrong position to fight the Welsh it may be that the fortification was started to meet the threat from the Vikings.

Whilst enjoying the walks the eye is often carried to the many humps and dips found throughout the whole area. These are the result of many centuries of mining for copper ore, traces of which can be found on the rock outcrops and in veins not far beneath the fallen leaves.

For many visitors the woods and paths are all they see but beneath their feet lies a very different world, out of sight and in most cases out of mind.

Members of the Derbyshire Caving Club can be occasionally spotted scurrying between their club house and the entrances to some of the many mine workings found under the Edge. Although largely unseen, the club is vital to the safety and accessibility of the whole area, securing many of the shafts and old entrances to the mines, which are so inviting, especially to groups of young people. In years gone by many adventurous explorers have fallen into danger when delving into the darkness under the Edge. There are at least nine areas of mine workings with evidence indicating that the area was worked as far back as the Bronze Age.

Some of the earliest workings known as Bell Pits were dug very close to the surface and consisted of a short shaft which was then widened at its base to follow the veins of ore. The great advantage of this type of working was its simplicity, which required little skill, at least in the initial stages, and did not require a great deal of manpower. The amount of ore which could be reached by this method was very limited. Traces of several of these pits can be found close to some of the footpaths. A similar method was used, much later, to extract coal on the Wirral Peninsula at Denhall. Due to the proximity of the surface, flooding could be a major problem. The Romans overcame some of the difficulties by sinking deeper shafts than those mined during the Bronze Age. The Romans have left considerable evidence of their mining work at Alderley and the standard of their work when cutting tunnels is very high.

A hoard of Roman coins was found in 1995 in a side chamber off a

The Wizard restaurant, Alderley Edge

deep shaft near to the Engine Vein Mine, which is one of the most obvious sites of mining activity found on the Edge.

One of the objects and desires of the Caving Club is to explore and secure the mines whilst obtaining as much information of their past as possible. There is evidence that the mines were used after the departure of the Romans but much of the evidence has been hidden by subsequent work during the 18th and 19th centuries. Vast chambers have been hewn from the rock by miners during this period who were able to proceed much deeper than the Romans by adopting the procedure of driving a drainage shaft into the base of the hill to release water and avoid flooding the working areas.

As the workings drove deeper below ground it became very difficult to extract the spoil and dispose of it on the surface. The obvious solution was to use the earlier workings to dispose of the spoil by backfilling the tunnels. Unfortunately this means that much of the evidence of the earliest work has been buried under the spoil of later workings. Shafts and evidence of further underground workings sometimes appear as rotten wooden covers give way and soil drops into old chambers.

One of the problems faced by the Caving Club is the loss, during a fire at nearby Alderley Park, of the plans of the mines. The plans were kept at the home of the Stanley family who owned the estate and their loss prevents many parts of the mine from being located. Although there may be copies of the plans in private hands obtaining a copy has so far proved impossible.

Alderley Edge is fascinating. Once the visitor can understand what lies under their feet they can understand and appreciate the true nature of what surrounds them. A cross inscribed on a stone near the Saddlebore mine is similar to others used to mark the boundaries of either parishes or estates. A casual glance at the Iron Age forts found on all similar rock outcrops in the county makes it almost certain that another lies at Alderley Edge.

Bronze Age burial mounds can be found in many places around Cheshire and neighbouring Derbyshire. Evidence found in the mines show that people of that age were living nearby whilst they extracted the copper. It is reasonable to expect that one or more of the many mounds on the Edge may contain burials from the neighbouring community.

Alderley Edge is a tribute to the work of both the National Trust and the Derbyshire Caving Club. The area is unique and visitors are welcome to explore in a sensible manner. The caving club open parts of the mines to visitors twice a year to raise money for the ongoing security of the old shafts.

Alderley Park, which lies in the shadow of The Edge, is now the property of the pharmaceutical company AstraZeneca. Before AstraZeneca, the property was the home of the Stanley family and their Eagle and Child crest can be found by the entrance gates.

One of the prominent members of the family was Lord Derby who during the First World War had a major role in raising the volunteers who rushed forward in response to an appeal from Lord Kitchener. The volunteers were formed into battalions known as "The Pals". These units were locally recruited so that friends could join, train and fight together. There were so many volunteers that the Army could not cope and, in the early months, these battalions were sponsored by the wealthy, who provided for all their needs, including uniforms, until the Army was able to receive them. Lord Derby sponsored several battalions from the Liverpool and Lancashire area with the men at first wearing silver cap badges of the Eagle and Child. When adopted by The Kings Liverpool Regiment they changed to the white horse of Hanover. Kitchener's "New Army" was probably the finest army ever to take the field. Every man was a volunteer and many had lied about their age to be accepted by "their" battalion.

At 7.30 a.m. 1st July 1916 the whistles blew and the troops went "over the top" on the first day of the Battle of the Somme. Although some of Kitchener's men had seen combat the previous year, the Somme was the first time they had fought together and most of the attacking force were "New" army troops. Believing that all the defences had been destroyed by the heaviest artillery barrage ever seen, they walked in neat lines towards the German lines. With rifles held "At the Port" and some units kicking footballs, they followed orders to the letter. Unfortunately the Germans had not been destroyed and their machine guns were in good order.

In that first day the British Army suffered over 57,000 casualties. The local nature of the battalions meant that whole families and towns were devastated and sounded the death knell of the concept.

The pride in their volunteer status felt by the soldiers is shown by my uncle's grave. Killed with so many others on the first day of the Somme he lies in the quiet fields of France under a stone bearing the Eagle and Child crest.

Lord Derby became the director general of recruiting producing the Derby Scheme, which introduced a previously unknown word to Britain - "conscription".

The Stanley family owned three public house near Alderley Park, the Wizard restaurant, the Black Greyhound on the Macclesfield road and the Eagle and Child opposite Alderley Mill. All three were disposed of after one of the family converted to Islam. A tall column bearing the Eagle and Child stands in the centre of a field on the estate and marks the last resting place of the only member of the Stanley family to have converted.

Chelford churchyard, some 2 miles from Alderley, has two graves, which are well worth a second look. A war grave records the death on May 6th 1916 of Private Abraham Street who died of cerebrospinal fever in the Isolation Hospital at Chester. Although there is no evidence to indicate that there was anything unusual in this tragic death, local belief is very different. The story, held by family and residents at the time, is that a doctor, who was later shot as a German spy, deliberately injected the young soldier with the disease.

A second grave bears testimony to a serious rail disaster in the village. Next to the church stands a memorial to Margaret Ellks and 13 others who died on 22nd December 1894 when a train crashed into equipment being used for maintenance work.

Christmas always seems to attract tragedy and on Boxing Day 1982 another rail crash at Minshull Vernon near Crewe killed 18 people.

Railway signals and maintenance procedures featured in the subsequent enquiry. Over a century after the Chelford crash the same questions arise following every disaster. Nothing changes.

The road from Chelford to Holmes Chapel passes the fields of Astle Park a lovely country house which normally enjoys the peace of the countryside. One weekend every August the scene is somewhat changed as the park is host to a steam rally with traction engines, tractors and vintage vehicles providing a wonderful day out for all ages. Visitors come from all over the county and enjoy a day when children are welcomed as an excuse for dad and grandfather to enjoy being young again.

It is not many years since two traction engines were being used to dredge the lake near to the hall. During the work a considerable number of bombs were found buried near the water. Issued to the Home Guard, they were intended to be used to stop German tanks in case of an invasion. I was present when they were prepared for detonation by the army and ever since I have had considerable respect for those who undertake such work.

Holmes Chapel lying close to the M6 motorway has expanded greatly in recent years but a small group of old cottages stand near the church. A serious fire in 1753 destroyed most of the old village. Previously known as Church Hulme, the name indicates a settlement by Danish Vikings probably originating from the east of the Pennines. Small indentations on the walls of the church are believed to be the results of musket balls fired during the civil war.

Fire Mark

The road from Holmes Chapel to Knutsford passes through Cranage, where a fine example of a Fire Mark can be found on a cottage near the turn-off for Twemlow. Fire Marks take the form of a plaque or plate featuring the logo of an insurance company and are usually found on the front wall of a house.

In the days before Fire Brigades were formed, putting out a fire was very much a case of "Do It Yourself".

Obviously, there were considerable problems in putting out a serious fire with only a bucket and a village pump, which could be some distance from the conflagration.

The earliest Fire Brigades were paid by the insurance companies and looked after the clients of those companies. If a house was on fire the brigade would attend, look for the Fire Mark and if the house was not insured, either go away, or sign up a new customer at a "Special" rate, before dealing with the blaze.

Shortly after passing the church at Toft another Fire Mark can be found fixed to a cottage on the right of the road whilst others can be found on many old buildings including "The Old Broken Cross", near Northwich, "The Swan", at Tarporley and in Abbey Square, Chester.

Byley is a tiny village situated on the minor road between Middlewich and Lower Peover. The village boasts a church, village hall, school and a building similar to a small warehouse.

Behind the church is a clue to the past. Rows of war graves are the last resting place of many airmen who died whilst stationed in the village during the Second World War. A few crumbling remains covered by grass are all that is left of the wartime aerodrome, which is now bisected by the M6 motorway. The industrial building was used during the war to build parts for Wellington bombers at a time when aircraft production was dispersed as protection against raids by the German airforce. Warmingham Mill between Middlewich and Crewe served a similar purpose.

Whenever I pass the building at Byley I ponder the fate of a "pickled" whale I last met in 1971. An astute business man had obtained the body of a large whale, preserved the corpse, and then mounted a whaling exhibition inside the body. Carried on a large articulated trailer, the whale toured the country, visitors were charged to enter the most bizarre display hall I have ever seen. Some years after viewing the exhibition, I had occasion to call at Byley and there at the back of the building was my old friend Jonah. I have always wondered what happened to him, or her!

Map References

Lindow Common: SJ 825814

Quaker Graves: SJ 807802

Chapter Ten

Roman Roads, Parachutes and Children's Stories

Knutsford, Tatton Park, Mere, Appleton Thorn, Thelwall, Wilderspool, Warrington, Daresbury and Runcorn

In Knutsford can be found the keys to reminders of war, literature, crime and religion.

The Charge of the Light Brigade at Balaclava is recalled by a plaque on the home of Trumpet Major William Smith, 1822-1879, who lived in Stanley Road. It was this soldier who sounded the charge in one of the most glorious "cock ups" in the history of the British army.

Nearby in Gaskell Avenue is the house of Edward Higgins the highwayman. In 1754 Higgins had been tried for housebreaking in Worcester and transported to America. Using money obtained from crimes in Boston, Higgins returned to England and in 1757 married Katherine Birtles at Knutsford. Higgins appears to have been a plausible character who would socialise with the local gentry except when visiting his estates. It later became clear what his business involved when he was convicted of crimes in Gloucester, Bristol and Carmarthen. Sentenced to death he produced an official pardon. Unfortunately the authorities realised that it was a forgery and in 1767 he was hanged after confessing to numerous crimes including murder. It is recorded that a Doctor White from Sale later obtained his skeleton for research.

To the casual observer the former home of Higgins looks perfectly normal. On closer inspection it can be seen that one of the upper windows is false. Complete with a real window frame, the wall has been painted to represent a window and so present a balanced, appearance. This method was used to avoid the financial penalty imposed by the window tax, a novel idea of Prime Minister William Pitt. It was the origin of the expression "Daylight Robbery". The ability of various Chancellors to raise tax from almost anything is a source of constant amazement.

The Sessions House, Knutsford

A few doors along the same road is the home of Elizabeth Gaskell who is well known for writing "Cranford", the story of a fictitious town based on Knutsford and using, as characters, people she had known. Elizabeth was born in Chelsea in 1810 but, when her mother died the following year, her aunt brought her up in Knutsford. Elizabeth married William Gaskell the Unitarian Minister at Knutsford but due to the ecclesiastical laws at the time the ceremony had to be held at Knutsford Parish Church.

Although Elizabeth died in Hampshire in 1865 she is buried in the grounds of Knutsford Unitarian Chapel.

In Princess Street close to the Parish Church, there is a set of stone stairs from which John Wesley preached to the people of Knutsford. This extraordinary man travelled miles preaching the gospel at a time when travelling even a short distance presented many difficulties.

For such a relatively small town Knutsford abounds in unusual buildings. One of the most prominent, the Sessions House in Toft Road, was originally part of a prison built in 1818 to hold 800 inmates. The building ceased to operate as a civilian prison before the First World War during which it was used to hold German Prisoners of War and conscientious objectors. After the Armistice Toc H used the buildings until the 1930s when most of the structures were

The Elizabeth Gaskell Tower, King Street, Knutsford

demolished. The present building houses a Magistrates court and a Court of Assize. Whilst delivering one of my slide presentations, I was delighted to learn that a large chip in the stone stairs at the entrance was caused by a bren-gun carrier chasing one of the audience during one of those lighter hearted moments in the middle of the Second World War.

Many of the residential and commercial buildings in Knutsford display a strong Italianate influence.

Richard Harding Watt, the son of a Manchester glove manufacturer certainly left his distinctive mark on the town. Buying as much land as possible, he built in a very different style to anything else found in Cheshire. The old main street is named King Street and the year 1907 saw a tower in memory of Elizabeth Gaskell built as part of a restaurant. Watt designed the distinctive Ruskin Rooms in 1900 as a recreation facility for the workers from his laundry.

Richard Watt always insisted on doffing his hat to the tower he had created to the memory of Elizabeth Gaskell. Unfortunately in 1913 he did this once too often causing his horse to bolt and throw him to the ground causing fatal injuries.

During the Second World War the Ruskin Rooms housed "The Doughnut Club" for officers on the staff of General "Blood and Guts" Patton who was stationed at Peover Hall. Patton was considered the obvious choice to lead the invasion of Europe and instead he was stationed at Knutsford in an effort to mislead the Germans. A United States flag hangs in Peover church, which stands next to the hall, commemorating the General's stay.

The narrow pavements at the start of King Street can be attributed to Lady Jane Stanley who insisted the pavement should be narrow to prevent immoral behaviour. Couples had actually been seen walking arm in arm!

At the northern end of King Street, Knutsford lies an entrance to Tatton Park, one of the most popular National Trust properties in Cheshire and visited by many thousands each year. The former home of the Egerton family is host to several national events and provides ample room for visitors to enjoy the grounds as well as the hall itself. Those who keep their eyes open may notice a modest stone set in the park land not far from the hall. This stone commemorates the many thousand people who "dropped in" to Tatton during the Second World War.

Manchester Airport, previously known as Ringway, was home to No 1 Parachute Training School. The airport is only a few miles from Tatton and provided an ideal situation whereby paratroops and others undergoing parachute training would be carried aloft from the airfield, jump over the Tatton estate and then be collected by lorry and returned to Ringway. Many of those who fought at Arnhem and other operations requiring the use of airborne forces completed their training at Tatton. That other brave band of men and women who were dropped behind enemy lines for special operations also trained here.

Tatton Park dates back many centuries and is the site of an Anglo Saxon settlement from between 700 and 800 years AD.

A motorist travelling from Knutsford towards Warrington will pass Mere Cross Roads and may catch a glimpse of a well preserved example of the old style AA phone boxes which were installed immediately after the last war. At that time boxes were provided to enable members to telephone for assistance and at the same time shelter from the worst of the elements. The modern emergency telephones may be more cost efficient but do not provide any protection and make any form of conversation impossible due to traffic noise. The box was one of the last examples in central England and provides a splendid example of not putting off until tomorrow what we can do today. Between deciding to photograph the box and attending at the scene the box was totally destroyed in a road accident. No trace of the original now remains and the present box is reproduction.

Besides the Parish Church at Appleton Thorn stands a tree enclosed by a small metal fence. Red ribbons can be found in the branches left from the ceremony of "Bawming the Thorn". The present tree, which dates from 1967, replaces other thorns which have occupied the same site since 1178.

The original tree, a cutting from the Glastonbury Thorn, was brought to the village by Adam de Dutton who was returning from the crusades.

The Glastonbury Thorn is reputed to have sprung from the staff of Joseph of Arimathea. The custom of "Bawming the Thorn" is believed to have originated in pagan rituals and was practised between 1178 and the late 19th century but then died out until revived in 1973.

The church clock at Stretton informs the traveller of more than the time of day. One face carries the words "Forget Not God", the other "Time Is Not All". The church overlooks a park, in the corner of which is a large statue of a Roman head. Two major Roman roads joined near here. The roads from Chester and Middlewich came to what is now Stockton Heath in order to cross the River Mersey at Wilderspool en route to Cocivm or Wigan. The actual crossing point was not far from the present road bridge but the river has changed course and has been subject to straightening during the period prior to the construction of the present canal system.

Wilderspool was not just a river crossing. In addition to stationing troops to protect the site, the Romans established what today would probably be called an industrial estate, producing metal, glass, leather and other commodities they required.

Rivers were a major problem for trade and military forces alike and had considerable strategic value. The Roman army and much later the Mercian armies, who faced the might of Northumbria across the river, both recognised the necessity of protecting the crossing point.

The Romans defended the crossing by establishing a fort close by at Thelwall which means "Wooden Walls".

Although in recent times Thelwall has become famous for the massive traffic jams which have occurred on the viaduct carrying the M6 motorway over the river, the village has its own place in history. In the year 923 King Edward the Elder founded a city here to protect the river crossing at Wilderspool in his wars against the invading Vikings. The fact is recorded in the Pickering Arms.

Perhaps Thelwall can lay claim to be the second city of Cheshire.

The departure of the Roman legions did not mean that Wilderspool ceased to be important. The crossing was not just of military importance, The combination of roads and river provided opportunities for trade and this was exploited to the benefit of the expanding town and industries which grew up in the area.

Warrington developed as a town with a selection of industries rather than having one dominant trade or business. Glass, leather, chemical and wire industries all grew here together with breweries. Although becoming part of modern Cheshire only in 1974, the town shared many experiences with the rest of the county.

The town museum displays a plague stone similar in construction to that found at Congleton.

Serious crime was also a problem here and in 1791 a post boy, James Hogworth, was murdered in Padgate and the post stolen. An Edward Miles was caught and put on trial for the crime. Found guilty, Miles was sentenced to hang and to be gibbeted for the offence. He was duly executed and his body taken to Padgate where it was encased in a steel cage and then hung until it rotted away as an example to others. Miles was the last person to be gibbeted in Warrington, this charming custom was only abolished in 1861. The gibbet cage can be seen in Warrington Museum.

Warrington boasts one of the most spectacular sets of front gates in the country. The gates were built in 1860 at Ironbridge, the centre of the Iron industry. Originally intended for the Royal estate at Sandringham, the Norfolk residence of Queen Victoria, they were purchased in 1895 by a Frederick Monks and finally found themselves in Warrington outside the house of the Patton family. The house and gates were later taken over by the council.

By the side of Upper Bridge Street, in the pedestrianised centre of the town is a plaque to the two young boys killed in an IRA bomb atrocity in 1993. It can only be hoped that such obscenities can become outdated and the decent people of Ireland and mainland Britain can live without fear from any faction.

Shipbuilding is not the industry, which comes to mind when visiting Warrington. Even allowing for changes to the width and flow of the river its appearance suggests that barges or small boats would be the limit of its capacity.

In 1854, the Clipper Ship *Tayleur* was constructed at Bank Quay. With a steel hull and powered by sail she was intended for the Australian run and at 1979 tons she was a large ship for her day. Hailed as unsinkable and with considerable publicity, this ship was owned by the White Star Line of Liverpool. Sailing on her maiden voyage with a promising future ahead *Tayleur* did not travel far before hitting rocks off the Irish coast. With a loss of over 300 lives, the tragedy was remarkably similar to that of the *Titanic* who was also "unsinkable", owned by the same company and on her maiden voyage. A commemorative stone to the *Tayleur* can be found at Dun Laoghaire near Dublin.

A glance at the weather vane on the village school at Daresbury can bring back the dreams of childhood. Charles Lutwidge Dodgson, better known as Lewis Carroll was born at the Parsonage in 1832. Although the Parsonage is no more, a memorial window in the Church and the weather vane which depicts the characters from *Alice in Wonderland* act as a reminder of one of the most famous writers of children's stories.

To the north of Daresbury the land falls away to the banks of the River Mersey with views of the town of Widnes and the power station at Fiddlers Ferry. Stretching across the river, towers the great span of the bridge between Runcorn and Widnes.

The River Mersey was traditionally the northern border of Cheshire, with Northumbria and then Lancashire on the far bank. The ford at Wilderspool and later the bridge at what had become Warrington provided the nearest crossing point to the sea. At the point where Runcorn faces Widnes, the river is still wide but below this point widens considerably.

Halton Castle: seat of the Constable of Cheshire

In 915, Queen Ethelfleda, daughter of King Alfred, had built a wooden fort at Runcorn in order to protect the gap leading to the fords at Wilderspool against attack by the Vikings. In 1071 the Normans also recognised the need to protect the gap and built Halton Castle to control this part of Cheshire. The Baron of Halton held the position of Constable of the county.

In 1115 monks of the St Augustine Order founded a house in Runcorn and in 1134 moved to the Priory at Norton. The ruins of the Priory are a popular location for school groups and others looking at this period in our history.

During the second half of the twentieth century the politicians and town planners decided, quite properly, that the standard of housing to be found in many of the cities was no longer acceptable.

Instead of improving the housing stock within the cities and keeping communities together, new town were created, or existing small towns used, as a nucleus for "overspill" from the cities.

The small town of Runcorn was greatly increased in size with whole communities transferred from Liverpool. The standard of housing was much better but the existing town was swamped under a mass of new building. The village of Halton, which lies in the shadow of the castle, provides a small but attractive window into the past.

Map References

Airborne Memorial: SJ 753819

Wilderspool: SJ 615865

Halton Castle: SJ 541821

Chapter Eleven

The Industrial Revolution and Modern Communications

Road and Canal Systems and the village of Hale.

Standing on the ridge alongside the walls of Halton Castle it is easy to see why Cheshire has played such a major role in the history of this country. The view takes in the approaches to the old river crossing at Wilderspool, the River Mersey, the Railways, the Manchester Ship Canal, the Bridgewater Canal, the Runcorn Widnes Bridge, the motorways, the Thelwall Viaduct and aeroplanes approaching and leaving both Liverpool and Manchester airports.

Cheshire remained important for both trade and external military purposes long after the end of the civil war. All trade with Ireland and all traffic between London and the North West had to pass through the county. Using our present-day eyes we forget the difficulties faced until very recently in providing basic transport. The Industrial Revolution could not have taken place using the old Roman roads or the system of unmade tracks which, for generations, had joined villages together. Goods often took days or even weeks to complete a long journey, with coaches and travellers both suffering the effects of jolting over pot holes and uneven surfaces. Only for those living near the coast was transporting goods by ship a practical proposition.

As the population of the country increased, the existing road system was totally incapable of meeting the needs of the country and some method had to be devised to improve the situation.

The problem was that nobody was really responsible for maintaining the highway. The Highways Act of 1555 made each parish responsible for the maintenance of the roads within its boundaries. Each household held to be worth over a certain value was to provide basic tools and workers for a prescribed number of days each year in much the same manner as the residents of Burton in Wirral were required to maintain their well and drinking water. Unfortunately whilst the residents would have a vested interest in their own health and water

The Bridgewater Canal at Lymm

supply, that did not apply to roads used by travellers. The system was not a success.

The first of the Turnpike Trusts was created in 1663. Each Trust was responsible for the maintenance of a section of highway and was empowered to levy a charge on those using the road. In theory the money raised would not only maintain the road but also improve and extend the road network. Some improvements were made but, as the Trusts existed to make a profit for members, only economically viable locations were considered. At first the Turnpikes were uncommon but, over the next century, the numbers increased until, by the mid 19th century, between 10 and 20 per cent of the main roads in Cheshire were managed by Turnpike Trusts. It is ironic that today the very same idea is being considered as a means of financing new roads without involving the government in the full cost. It is not only wheels that travel in circles!

The introduction of long-distance coaches took place in 1637 with a coach service joining Birmingham, Nantwich, Chester and Holywell. Twenty years later in 1657 a service started between London and Chester. This was later extended to Holyhead.

The start of the Industrial Revolution meant that communications and an efficient transport system was becoming increasingly necessary. In practice the Turnpikes were not capable of meeting the changing social and economic circumstances and the development of the country was being retarded by the condition of the roads.

Following the Jacobite rebellion of 1715 General George Wade improved some roads to enable the army to be deployed more efficiently. Between 1815 and 1830 the new A5 London to Holyhead road was constructed. Surveyed by that great engineer Thomas Telford, this vital road no longer passed through Cheshire but did set new standards for road construction. The involvement of such engineers as Telford and the development of the tarmacadam surface in 1826, revolutionised the whole approach to road building. These factors created the conditions, which would enable the road system to meet the requirements of the internal combustion engine.

In Cheshire the creation of a practical method of building roads would lead inevitably to the present-day road network and the Thelwall Viaduct. The viaduct, which opened in 1963, is 4427 feet long and with its 36 arches carries the M6 motorway over the river and the Manchester Ship Canal providing a vital link between the north and south of the country.

If the road system could not yet cope with the needs of business then an alternative had to be found and one soon appeared. As the most efficient way of carrying goods was by water it was decided to take the water to the factories. It was the age of the canals and Cheshire played a very important role. At first, existing rivers were straightened to ease the passage of boats. These were called 'Navigations' with Acts of Parliament for the River Weaver and the River Mersey and Irwell Navigations being passed in 1720. The new waterways were of great assistance in the movement of salt and related products from Cheshire to newly developed markets.

The first artificial canal was built in Newry, Northern Ireland and in Cheshire the Sankey canal, which formed part of the St Helens canal, had been constructed in 1757 to carry coal from St Helens to Liverpool and Cheshire. In 1759 an Act of Parliament was passed authorising the construction of one of the first wholly artificial waterways to carry goods from Manchester to near Runcorn where it entered the River Mersey. This canal was engineered by James Brindley, who had carried out his apprenticeship at Macclesfield. It was named after the Duke of Bridgewater who had financed the venture.

The Bridgewater Canal heralded a period of canal building which created a network of canals joining many parts of the country and leading to the developments of new towns which could now be joined to the sea. Ellesmere Port was one example of the new towns.

Revolutionary in their day, the canals did not lead the technological race for long as the Railway Age soon followed. The Stockton to Darlington Railway became the world's first passenger carrying railway soon followed by the Manchester and Liverpool Railway in 1830.

If Cheshire had witnessed one of the first canals it also was host to one of the last of the major canal projects in this country. In 1885 an Act of Parliament was passed authorising the construction of the Manchester Ship Canal. The canal was intended to enable large ships to load and unload their cargo in Manchester itself and so dispense with the need to use the facilities of the Port of Liverpool. There was initial opposition from Liverpool, who obviously saw the project as a competitor and the supporters of both cities employed considerable influence before the Act was passed. Work started in November 1887 with Daniel Adamson of Didsbury providing the driving force until his death in 1887. Lord Egerton of Tatton then became chairman.

The first section of the canal opened to traffic in 1891. Construction of the remainder was completed in December 1893 and brought into use on 1st January 1894. Queen Victoria officially opened it in May 1894. The canal was 35.5 miles long with five sets of locks and cost £15m.

The effect of the canal was not restricted to Manchester. The town of Ellesmere Port developed to handle cargo between sea going ships and the narrow boats using the Ellesmere Canal. Before the opening of the Manchester Ship Canal, the largest ship to reach the port was restricted to about 400 tons laden, the canal changed that situation overnight.

The canals and the railways provided an essential means of moving raw materials and finished products between factory and markets. For the majority of the population movement by road was still a real problem and crossing the River Mersey required either a boat trip or a diversion to the crossing at Warrington.

For many years consideration was given to building a bridge across the river between Runcorn and Widnes. In the early part of the 19th century Telford proposed a 1000ft suspension bridge which would have provided a 20ft wide roadway and given 70 feet of clearance at high water. However it was not until the dawn of the railway age that the first bridge was built. Between 1863 and 1868 The London and North West Railway Company constructed the present railway bridge across the river.

By the end of the 19th century it was clear that some means of crossing the river had to be provided for passengers not using the railway. In 1905 a 1000ft transporter bridge was opened at a cost of £137,663. Suspended from a lattice of girders, a platform approximately 55ft long and 24ft wide could carry about 12 cars and 300 passengers across the river in three minutes. On its opening day 2000 passengers were carried across in one hour.

The development of motor transport required a more effective means of crossing the river and in July 1961 the present bridge was opened. With a total span of 1082ft and a cost of £2.9 million the basic concept sounds remarkably similar to that proposed by Telford so many years ago.

The Child of Hale

Across the river and almost hidden behind the expanse of Liverpool Airport lies the village of Hale. Since 1974 the locals have found themselves part of Cheshire although few people in Cheshire seem to realise that they have gained an extremely attractive addition to the county. Black and white cottages with thatched roofs accompany the parish church, which is host to and overlooked by, a most unusual person.

Visitors to the church are bound to notice a large figure standing alongside the road. Carved from the trunk of a tree, the likeness of John Middleton, who was known as the Child of Hale, has immediate impact. The most famous resident of the church yard, John Middleton was born in 1578 and grew to an astonishing nine feet three inches. He is remembered not only by the carving and his grave but also by the village inn, which carries his picture and title.

Map References

Hale Church: SJ 471820

Chapter Twelve

The Centre of the County

Northwich, Bostock, Great Budworth, Little Budworth, Eddisbury, Delamere and Nunsmere.

Geographically, Northwich is the nearest town to the centre of the county and not far away is the village of Bostock. New roads have removed much of the traffic which used to flow between Middlewich and Davenham but by the side of the road and near the village hall is an impressive tree marking the actual centre of the county prior to the 1974 boundary changes.

Salt has long been important in the history of Northwich and has formed the basis of its wealth over the years. Many large chemical companies have sites in the town and the River Weaver has been made navigable to enable salt and the products of the local industry to be carried to the Manchester Ship Canal and hence to the sea.

The extraction of salt in the form of brine has not been without cost. Over the years a considerable number of buildings in the town

The Town Bridge, Northwich

have subsided and many of the older buildings were constructed in such a manner that they could be jacked up to overcome problems. The old Post Office, now a restaurant, is the largest building constructed in this manner and stands four storeys high.

The River Weaver passes close to the centre of the town and is crossed by two unusual bridges. Town Bridge and its neighbour Hayhurst Bridge are both electric-powered swing bridges. Three-fifths of the weight is carried by floating pontoons to overcome subsidence. Town Bridge, which was the first to be completed in 1899, is the oldest electrically powered swing bridge in the world.

At the dawn of the 21st century, local football enthusiasts were still able to watch the Victoria Football Club play at the oldest Football Association ground in the world. The same ground has been played continually by the same club since 1874. Unfortunately commercial interests make it unlikely that the use of the area for football will continue. Prior to football, the ground was the drill field of the 22 Company, 3rd Battalion, Cheshire Rifle Volunteers.

On the outskirts of Northwich lies Winnington. On 19th August 1659 a battle occurred between Sir George Booth on the Royalist side and General Lambert for Parliament. The battle appears to have covered a considerable area as it started near Hartford and is claimed as the last battle of the civil war. There is some argument about whether the incident should be classified as a battle or a mere skirmish and the final judgement lies with historians. It was reported that Sir George Booth was detained leaving the field disguised as a woman.

Within half a mile of Winnington bridge lies the Anderton Boat Lift. Constructed in 1875 to carry barges between the Trent and Mersey canal and the River Weaver, the lift designed by Edwin Clark, was the first of its type in the world with later versions in both France and Belgium. Originally using hydraulics, the lift was converted to electric power between 1906 and 1908. Prior to the lift, cargo chutes, a tramway and two inclined planes were used to carry goods between the two waterways. Concern over the safety of the structure resulted in the lift being closed in 1983. After many years trying to raise the necessary funds, financial assistance has been obtained from the European Community and an extensive restoration programme has restored this monument of Victorian engineering expertise lift to its former glory. Weaverham, which lies downstream from Northwich, was the court and prison for the Abbey at Vale Royal.

Alongside the Northwich to Runcorn Road at the junction with the road to picturesque Great Budworth lies a small structure resembling a church lychgate. This is a well house, constructed in 1880 to protect the village water supply and it remained in use until 1934. The water

Awaiting restoration: the Anderton Boat Lift

supply was generally thought to be of good quality and the residents from local villages would journey to collect their needs. Unfortunately on one occasion, a subtle change in flavour which had proved extremely popular, was traced to a nearby donkey that had expired some time earlier!

The Old Well House, Great Budworth

At the end of the 19th century one of the most popular attractions was the "Wild West" show with Buffalo Bill, who had made his name and fortune on the American frontier during the Indian wars. Buffalo Bill toured with many famous Indians including Sitting Bull, who was probably the best known of all the Indian chiefs. Buffalo Bill stayed at Forest Hill near Sandiway when he visited Liverpool in 1890 and is reported as having ridden with the Cheshire Hunt.

Travellers using the A556

Manchester to Chester road at Sandiway pass a small round sandstone tower standing uncomfortably in the centre of the dual carriageway. It was built in the early years of the 19th century as a gate house for the Vale Royal estate. Inhabited until the 1920s the existing structure provided the main accommodation with a small extension acting as a single bedroom.

The Blue Cap Hotel, a few hundred yards towards Chester, is named after a foxhound that, in 1763, won a race in which he and his daughter raced against two Quorn hounds. The owner of Blue Cap, John Smith-Barry was the first Master of Foxhounds for the Cheshire Hunt, which is based at Sandiway. The stakes between the owners is recorded as 500 guineas.

Nunsmere Hall can be found close to Sandiway alongside the A49 road. The hall was built around 1900 for Sir Aubrey Brocklebank, chairman of the Brocklebank Shipping Line, which originated in the early 18th century. The company and its ships played an important role during the First World War when food and other essential supplies had to be carried across the Atlantic despite the German U Boats. After the war the Brocklebank Line merged with Cunard and Sir Aubrey was involved in the planning for a new passenger liner which later became the *Queen Mary*. In 1963 his son John was chairman of Cunard at the time *Queen Elizabeth 2* was being designed.

Business of a different nature is illustrated by the Cabbage Hall public house near Sandibrow. The name has nothing to do with vegetables but is a term connected with tailors and the usage of cloth. An early inn keeper is reported to have come to the attention of the excise men after it was noticed that his donkey, whilst thin during the day, became quite rotund during the hours of darkness. The enterprising owner had made a comfortable waistcoat for the animal. Not for keeping the animal warm but to conceal contraband!

Close to Sandibrow lies Oulton Park, formerly a country house but now echoing to the roar of cars and motor cycles using the racing circuit situated within the grounds. Within the shadow of Oulton Park lies Little Budworth with a splendid pinfold by the roadside. This pinfold is slightly larger than that situated at Capenhurst.

Oulton Park lies close to what is now the southern limits of Delamere Forest. Although this old forest is now only a shadow of its former self it still provides valuable recreation for many who value the peace and tranquillity of the trees and pools. At Christmas the festive tree can be bought from those thinned from the forestry stock.

Oakmere Hall, Sandiway

Today the forest is very highly regarded but in the past it was not nearly so well regarded by the common folk of Cheshire.

The Normans established several forests within the county: Wirral, Macclesfield, Mara and Mondrem. Now known as Delamere, Mara would have born only the very slightest resemblance to the existing forest in either appearance or purpose. An area was declared a forest to ensure that the hunting was preserved for the Lords. Instead of rows of conifers, as are found today, the ground would have been heath land with small woods consisting of oak and other native trees ideal for supporting deer, wild boars and similar prey. Very strict laws applied in the forest to preserve the game. The right to gather wood, feed cattle and pigs or gather honey, were all restricted and the penalty for contravention harsh.

About three miles on the Manchester side of Kelsall and near the junction of the A556 and B5152 roads is the Iron Age fort of Eddisbury. In the early morning or late evening when the light casts shadows across the fields, ramparts and banks can still be clearly seen near the crest of the hill. The fort overlooks the old Roman road between Chester and Northwich and at the time of its construction must have been a formidable position. The outline of the fort is still visible, but most of the structure was destroyed at or near the time of the Roman occupation. At the time of the Viking incursions in 914

Eddisbury was re fortified along with several other Celtic Forts to provide a defence against the seaborne invaders. There is a clear line of sight between Eddisbury and neighbouring forts enabling mutual support to be readily available in time of need. The nearest fortification is at Helsby overlooking the marshes and the Wirral peninsula.

A walk along the sandstone ridge from Helsby to Frodsham, which is believed to have been the site of another fort, is especially invigorating on a windy day. The view across to the River Mersey and Wirral, like that afforded from Maiden Castle, provides the opportunity for enemies to be seen in ample time for plans to be prepared for engagement, or withdrawal if the enemy was too strong.

In the sandstone outcrops of the ridge, there is "graffiti" in the form of the names of lovers and individuals who have enjoyed this place. Some lettering is of outstanding quality and dates from 1862 or earlier. It may be that a walker can find their grandfather's name carved next to grandmother's, or maybe someone else's grandmother!

The remains of Kelsborrow Castle, another Iron Age fort, are to be found near Kelsall. From there the view opens to reveal Chester and the chimneys of Stanlow Oil Refinery. Although the scene is usually one of tranquillity, spoilt only by the intrusions of industry and the motorways, things have not always been as law-abiding as they seem.

In April 1796 a trial was held at Chester Assizes which was remarkably similar to that of Edward Miles at Warrington in 1791. James Price and Thomas Brown were charged with assaulting and robbing a post boy, Peter Yoxall, aged 15 years, on Tuesday 19th January 1796, at Thornton-le-Moors near what is now the refinery. Peter Yoxhall was carrying the mail and theft of the Royal Mail is still regarded as a very serious offence. The two men were arrested in Gosta Green, Birmingham, on 22nd January and returned to Chester for trial. Both Price and Brown, whose real name was apparently Smallman, were about 26 years old. Found guilty, they were hanged on April 30th 1796 and their bodies hung in chains at Trafford Green near to the scene of the offence.

Map References

Anderton Boat Lift: SJ 648753

Well House, Great Budworth: SJ 661774

Concluding Thoughts

Cheshire is a fascinating county. We can walk around and just see the present time. Dawn over the Pennines or sunsets across the Dee Estuary are equal to anywhere in the world. Although the beauty of Cheshire is wonderful, it is only when we consider our past and think of the famous names that have also walked this place do we really appreciate our heritage. The finest engineers of their time left their calling card. Telford, Brindley, Brunel and Stephenson left us an invaluable means of communication whilst the mightiest of Kings have made indelible impressions on our society. Keys to the past are all about us whether in physical form or in the spoken word.

From my home in Holmes Chapel I make a great many slide presentations to social groups throughout Cheshire and the surrounding counties. Although I obviously give out many facts about the subject of the presentation, on almost every occasion I gather some detail, however minor, from the audience. These snippets of information are invaluable but will be lost unless we encourage everybody, especially the elderly, to share and record their knowledge.

Provided we communicate with each other and make a conscious effort to look around us, we can open the door to a fascinating world which is there just waiting to be discovered.

Bibliography

A History of Cheshire: Alan Crosley

Cheshire: Fred H. Crossley. Robert Hale, 1949

A History of Cheshire: Dorothy Sylvester. Darwen Finlayson, 1971

Portrait of Cheshire: David Bethell. Robert Hale Ltd, 1979

Portrait of Chester: David Bethell. Robert Hale Ltd, 1980

Portrait of Wirral: Kenneth Burnley. Robert Hale Ltd, 1981

Cheshire and its Welsh Borders: Herbert Hughes. Dennis Dobson, 1966

The Forgotten Shores: Hope, 1988

Cheshire Curiosities: Peter Bamford. Dovecote Press, 1992

Cheshire, Its Magic and Mystery: Doug Pickford. Sigma Leisure, 1994

The Bog Man and the Archaeology of People: Don Brothwell. British Museum Press, Howard University Press, 1986

Hilbre, The Cheshire Island: Edited by J.D. Cragg. Liverpool University Press, 1982

Old Cheshire Churches: Raymond Richards. E.J. Morten, 1973

Thetis – "The Admiralty Regrets": Warren & Benson. Avid Publications, 1997

The Wirral Peninsula: Norman Ellison. Robert Hale Ltd, 1955

Chelford – A Cheshire Village: Plant, Roycroft and Slater, 1999

A Journey Through Time: Intec Publishing, 1996